[Handwritten inscription:]

Dr
W.
to your confident
but thoughtful
leadership
Sophie

THE ART OF THE CHIEF EXECUTIVE

Sophie Churchill has held four chief executive roles, leading small organisations with big causes and working across specialisms. Her love of Britain, its communities and its landscapes is deep, her perspectives also influenced by family and other ties to Africa, the Middle East and China. Sophie received an OBE for services to the environment in 2011 and has a PhD based on the lives of people with learning disabilities in long-stay hospitals. She enjoys mentoring leaders at all stages of their careers. For more information, see www.sophiechurchill.com.

SOPHIE CHURCHILL

The Art of the Chief Executive

A guide for aspiring and reflective leaders

ISBN 978-0-9956757-0-4

Contents

Foreword

I've written this book for anyone interested in the art, practice and daily rollercoaster of being a chief executive: what seems to work, how it feels, how to be happy doing it. I hope it is useful for prospective, new and established chief executives, their deputies, senior managers, chairs and all those whose waking hours are affected by the boss's approach, including the indispensable PAs of every organisation. If you have a hunch that one day you might be a chief executive, I hope it makes the prospect less daunting and more real. Equally, if you are keeping well out of the fray and are simply a student of management, I hope the lived-in and of course idiosyncratic perspective of one chief executive adds to the many excellent volumes and resources on leadership and management.

The book is structured around the dynamics of a chief executive role, from applying for your first chief executive post to your departure, and explores from my own lived experience, with anecdotes and examples from the experience of others, many of the standard topics you are likely to find in the management literature. But here you will read more of the thought processes, the practicalities and the things I should have done more or less of, rather than encounter a theoretical framework. At its core, unashamedly, is my belief that good business sits well with, rather than cuts across, the fair and thoughtful leader and vice versa. Here and there I draw on some of my areas of interest, including forestry and yoga, where they have helped make sense of being a chief executive, and strengthened me. Whatever one's preferences for keeping well – and I am prepared to accept that possibly the world does not need *that* many forester yogis – the book touches on the importance of staying physically and mentally content and fit. Well-being, whilst largely generated outside working hours, can certainly be jeopardised during them.

When my daughter was about fifteen, we went to a lengthy film about a family wedding going awry. I came out more enamoured of it than she was. After I expressed enthusiasm she sighed tolerantly and said 'Well, yes, I guess the oldest stories always bear repetition'. So here I'm taking her at her word – and hoping my lens brings some new insights on challenges you may have read about, or experienced from a distance. If you sit down with the book and a drink after a taxing and lonely week, or perhaps as you toy with a chief executive application, and you derive some strength from it, it will have achieved its purpose.

I've used the term 'chief executive' throughout, by which I essentially mean the executive boss of an organisation or business. That person might also be called the director, managing director, or some other term, depending upon the type of organisation and the conventions of the sector in which it operates. I also use many of the standard business terms, such as assets, customers, products and investments. Even though in my roles I have not been in manufacturing or indeed selling a product in the usually understood sense, I have found these concepts to be very useful and if they feel initially alien to you I would encourage you to translate them into your own context.

I have though had my fill of management books enlivened with photos of handshakes and purportedly universal theories of leadership. This book does not ask you to fill in exercises at the end of each chapter or to follow a prescribed course of activities or reflection. I hope it will simply give you moments of recognition or indignation, new insights and the reassurance of being accompanied in your journey into the art and craft of the chief executive. I wish you all reward and satisfaction in pursuing your vocation to lead. Or, if you are reading the book because it is your vocation to be led, I hope it is by people who know themselves, keep learning the art and who believe they aren't alone.

Dedication

I have worked with, and continue to work with, great people; the book is dedicated to them and their journeys as professionals and as human beings. They have witnessed close up that the advice of this book has not always been taken by its author. Thanks for sharing, teaching, mopping up around me and giving me joy.

Remembering Oliver Rackham

As I was writing this book we lost the great Oliver Rackham, ecologist and charter of the English countryside. I suspect that being a conventional chief executive would have been, for him, the ultimate penance, although he was, for a time, Master of an Oxbridge College. (As it happens I show, in the course of this book, how idiosyncratic that is as a leadership role). He was a great distiller of erudition for a wide audience and a fine leader of thought and practice. I invoke his trenchant spirit of enquiry after the often unfashionable truths:

'... *the subject* [the popular history of trees and woods] *has suffered from a long tradition of plagiarization and an unusually extensive corpus of folk-mythology'. Oliver Rackham*

Preface to 'Trees and Woodland in the British Landscape', First Edition, J.M. Dent, 1976.

I love the assumption in this typically ironic sentence, that *some* folk-mythology is to be expected, but that it is unacceptably extreme, in this case. Whether in a wood or an office, we could do worse than to follow Professor Rackham's approach, meticulously observing and discerning 'what the land itself, and the things that grow on it, have to say'.

9

Thanks

Whilst the book is based largely on my own experience, it has benefited immensely from conversations with many other people. My specific thanks go to the pseudonymous Robert, (Head of an Oxbridge college), Tricia, (chief executive of an environmental charity), Geoff, (head of operations and partner in a global automotive company), Frances (chief executive of a large national membership organisation), and William (former public sector chief executive, director of his own company and chair of a hospital trust). Their willingness to share the stretch points is to their credit and the great benefit of the book.

Thanks to Clive Cockerton, who improved the quality of the final draft and offered encouragement when most needed.

Finally, and most significantly of all, I'm blessed with inspiration and encouragement from Owen, Ben and Emily, my offsprung, in pursuing this project amongst others. The Mothership orbits gratefully around them and those they love.

Introduction: What is it to be a chief executive?

It has been a surprise and a pleasure in my working life to have been a leader of a number of organisations. That is to say, on a daily basis I have been called to show direction, wade through the daily treacle and gaze at the horizon, all at the same time and with as much poise as I can muster. It's been more than fun; I have been the one with the most varied diary, the most trips to interesting places and the most photos in which to smile.

It is hard to express what this privilege is like. Sometimes it can be a physical feeling in the belly, or a specific thought; I have often said to myself on arriving at the car park in the morning 'Goodness, all these people have got up and come to work today, *again!* Okay, it's up to me to make that seem like a good thing to do, not just something they have to do to pay the bills'. It is surprising, too, when the emotion kicks in, sometimes at most unexpected moments. I have always been ridiculously elated after a fire practice when the whole team has got out of the pseudo-inferno and the systems have worked, not relying on me. I've whispered 'Great, this team can look after itself'. I have had that belly feeling again when signing off annual accounts, each figure representing countless emails and conversations by colleagues, resulting in real change for the people we serve.

So, what is the job? It is to make the most of every resource, the least of every risk, and to secure the future. It is to amplify what the organisation stands for and reinforce its purpose and values, through the things you are seen to do and how you say the things you need to say. Its starting point is listening, its full manifestation then revealed in your eyes, your shoulders, your mouth and your feet.

You are the representative, the focal point, the hub of many and various efforts and very often the strongest association anyone outside the company makes with it, unless you are fortunate enough to have a very well-established inanimate brand, such as HP Sauce, or unfortunate enough to have an omnipresent chair or patron who wants the limelight. Doing this role well, you will find yourself preoccupied with three big significant chunks of activity and thought: legacy, people, and advocacy.

Firstly, your main legacy will be the long-term future, not day-to-day triumphs. To make this more concrete when in the daily hurly-burly, I have always tried to articulate with some precision, what would constitute a stronger position when I leave. This could for example be the asset base, income streams, customer base, or a wider reputation. I say more on this throughout the book, including in the chapter on 'leaving before you arrive'. Somehow, week by week, this future position has to be consciously in your mind, whether or not you have an immediate crisis to deal with. This provides the lens through which you look at budgets, structure, strategy and priorities of your team. It will be a great ally when you need to make unpopular decisions and, on your retirement day, it will be what shows you made a difference. In exceptional circumstances, of course, your legacy will have been to close down the company or organisation. Even if that is your lot, you will want to have done even this apparently miserable task to the best of your abilities.

Secondly, the organisation's main asset, in making sure there is indeed a future, is its people and you are there to make the most of them, day in and day out. Throughout this book I contend that leadership and management are interdependent elements of the same role, and a chief executive cannot but be exercised by the quality of management throughout the organisation, whether you are hands-on with your senior team or have an operational deputy who does most of its line management. This book is based on my experience of handling both internal and external relations in the chief executive role, but even if much of the internal management role is delegated to a chief operating officer, you are ultimately accountable to the board for the performance and efficiency of your staff and should have oversight of all major change processes. You also have a number of key relationships to manage directly yourself, including with your board. What this book emphasises is the need to flex your style and approach to cover the myriad experiences of management: getting the right people in, encouragement and guidance, getting some people out if necessary, coaching, listening to confidences, leading from the front, staying at the back, taking lunch with a colleague.

At the very least, chief executives should not be blocking people from doing the great things of which they are capable. The Chief

Education Officer in post when my children were his charges in Birmingham said that formal education's main task was not to get in the way of the normal learning embodied in every child. I wonder if we dare to believe that the role of a chief executive is similar; we shouldn't start with a pathological view that all organisations are on the edge of the abyss, even if some of what follows is about keeping yours far enough back from the edge.

Thirdly, you are the main advocate for and the external face of the organisation. Neither of the two priorities above should stop you from being seen out and about with key partners, building the loyalty of customers, or making sure that media coverage is as you'd like it. This needs a tricky mix of being proactive and structured, but also being willing to respond to the immediate opportunity, despite internal demands. In my roles, I have sometimes felt resistant to an afternoon spent feeding local media, knowing that I would then have to do write a paper later in the evening. I have spent whole days at meetings convened by partners and funders when only some of it was of direct benefit to my organisation, because I found that generosity with my diary and expertise was repaid in the long-term. However, I am unsure if, over my career as chief executive, I consistently focussed enough on the external face of the organisation and protected enough diary time just to do this. I say more about this in chapter seven.

If those are the three main chunks of the job, how has it felt and what is 'normal' to feel? Most days I have been happily adding to what is already strong and good. I have been fortunate in the causes I have been served and in the people around me. But to be honest, fairly regularly I have not been so far from the fraying, lonely edge and affecting others around me by being there. A seasoned chief executive can, on one of those days, still push forward on the agreed priorities, chair meetings and get the tasks done. But one of the burdens of self-aware leadership is knowing that what impacts on your team is not just what you say and do, but many things much less definable, yet not so hard to pick up. This might be the stiffness in your jaw or shoulders when stressed, avoiding a conflict which needs resolving or leaving out the softer communication with immediate colleagues which would oil the wheels of other conversations that will need to be had along the line. Perhaps the intractable work issues are beginning to etch themselves on your skin. Perhaps you haven't quite managed to keep the encroaching concerns of the rest of your life from sitting with you at your desk. Despite the rewards, there are many moments for the chief executive when you are stretched in your very sense of self. I would be doing you a disservice to make light of this, but equally these times are to be expected and the loneliness and fear are normal, not a failure. They are also, paradoxically, since by their nature they seem so individual and isolating an experience, shared by all leaders at some time.

I know of one chief executive of a local authority, in the midst of romantic nightmares, who had to say to his PA: 'I'm not good today. I need protection', and his PA tactfully kept the persistent elected members at bay. Here's to all the great and intuitive PAs who make the tough days possible. Similarly, I hope the pages following will help chief executives feel that they are accompanied, that when you are against the end of the plank, up and down the land many others are too, and next week will probably be different. Surely the sense of imperfection in the leadership role is what we should expect, and, if so, the accompanying flutters of the stomach can be greeted with equanimity. *Ultimately*, the question is not what you feel, but how to do your best – and I say this as someone who believes that feelings, even the least pleasant ones, are both guides and gifts to which we should pay heed.

My last most recent chief executive role was with the National Forest Company. With a wide range of partners, it is regenerating 200 square miles of England's Midlands affected by mining and other industries, which have left their scars on communities and landscapes. This transformation is being brought about through trees, which are great multifunctional bits of kit. With a number of strong leaders over its lifetime to date, the National Forest Company is very successful – and, you might imagine, not very controversial.

However, forestry does have its controversies, let me assure you. Probably the most contested word in the environmental sector is 'nature' or perhaps 'natural'. Walk into a woodland from the edge of a town or village and we breathe out and feel we are back in a 'natural' setting. But even a very old woodland is likely to have been planted, encouraged and shaped by humans. In fact, the older it is the more likely it is to have survived precisely because of its usefulness, and having been worked; foresters are very fond of the adage, 'The wood that pays is the wood that stays'. Many woodlands historically would have been places of more noise and activity than today, with shortish, coppiced trees grown and harvested for sticks, rather than ancient oaks, possibly with the smell of charcoal wafting through.

So, across all habitats and landscapes in the UK there is virtually nothing 'natural' to be found, in the sense of wild or untouched and, for better for worse, human beings have shaped what we now see and enjoy as countryside. Today's forester will continue that intervention rather than conserve something static; not too romantically, he or she will likely have a management plan, know the soil and orientation of the land, have a system to measure the growth and 'yield' of the maturing trees and will have to have some way of funding the work needed. Those quintessential English bluebells may have been planted just two years ago as part of a 'biodiversity plan'. Moreover, the forester will revel in a language peculiar to the forestry world ('beating up' being the replacement of young trees which have died, for example). We are talking science, jargon, techniques and numbers.

But at the same time, a good forester has real vision and heart for any site, along with years of learning gently wafting round the semi-conscious. He or she will know that you could actually justify many different choices based on gut preference, whilst claiming learned reasons for them. Compare this with any experienced gardener who will recognise what a relief it is to get to the point of just knowing that a particular plant will go well here. We can then become artists as well as technicians.

Similarly, the role of a chief executive is not just about a set of technical competencies, reinforced by constant self-analysis, mentoring, reading books like this one, or guru-immersion. But neither is it enough just to be at ease with oneself, relaxing and trusting intuition and experience. I have sometimes busked along merrily, indulging my own personality preferences, only to make some elementary blunder; other times I have been fed by some managerial tome or online article or, indeed, wisdom caught in the wind from a colleague, only to feel dissatisfied by my retention and application of that learning.

Somehow we need to find the impulse to carry on learning, without either complacency or, alternatively, extreme self-criticism and an unhelpful level of perfectionism. It has always surprised and encouraged me that some of the most famous of writers have attended classes, presumably scrubbing things out at the last minute and feeling nervous reading out their work to others. Our doodles in a protracted meeting are nothing compared with the reworkings of the manuscripts of most famous writers. Chief executives too learn and refine their art; our style will always be our own but we can amend it in the course of our lives or within a post as needed, with self-awareness and the help of others.

When we work reflectively on our style, some kind of alchemy might just take place between technical knowledge, remembered and unremembered experience and a heightened ability simply to respond to the situations in front of us with intelligence, equanimity and compassion. John Ruskin described the balance of brain and heart thus: 'He only is advancing in life whose heart is getting softer, whose blood warmer, whose brain quicker, whose spirit is entering Living Peace'. (Education and Life, Chapter 21).

Your expectation *should* be that you will get better and better at what you do. But a word of warning about power might be pertinent here. Never believe you're THAT good, just pretty good. Promotion and recognition pose dangers to the self. William, a chair of a hospital trust, running his own business and a chief executive early on in his professional life, says: 'Things that feed a sense of importance are very dangerous.' His professional journey subsequent to his early leadership role has been in part to check the potentially toxic effects of being known to be effective at an early age, a 'natural' leader who proved himself in a number of settings. He now allows himself to ask how he might actually be more deeply effective, more humble (or perhaps simply less certain) and yet using the power he undeniably has in the cause of, in his case, public service.

For others it is the reverse, having to overcome feelings of inadequacy early on and grow in confidence so as not to underplay the skills they have. This might apply to women more than men, to those who have not gone through the most mainstream and prestigious universities and those who have absorbed the message that they are not quite top material. That is quite a few people, many of whom will make thoughtful, brave leaders with masses of integrity. Mandela told us not to be afraid of our strengths; the quest is to find them, befriend them, mould them.

As a reminder that we are good, but not that good, the essays of Montaigne, a 16th century French nobleman who prefered writing to managing his estates, or the public life, are excellent dipping-into material for the chief executive at the end of a long day. They are shot through with the experience of a soldier, a landowner, a scholar. He was read in his lifetime, a period of great turbulence and violence in French history. He was successful. He overcame his fear of death when he once nearly died and felt a detached peace. (This incident was caused by misjudged overtaking on the part of a young horseman in Montaigne's retinue. Montaigne thought they were being attacked by bandits and sounds rather disappointed that it was just a youth not in control of his vehicle: *plus ça change*).

Yet he also says he does not know his mind from one moment to another and hates his indiscipline and idleness, his impatience of detail. But his willingness to say that, given his track record and erudition, allows us to walk more confidently in his wake. Perhaps in the end the place to be *is* oscillating regularly between feelings of competence and incompetence, confidence and fear, knowledge and ignorance – and to accept this as the normal background noise. Best however (too late to advise Montaigne who died in 1592) not to waste time berating ourselves for our shortcomings but to smile on our inevitably confusing self and get on with taking the opportunities for good every day. That would do nicely.

In yoga there is one particular pose, or asana, which I shared with my team at the National Forest Company; unsurprisingly, the 'tree' pose, or Vrksasana. You stand on one leg, the knee of the other bent to the side and the foot on the shin, thigh or tucked into the hip, (this last actually the most stable option). Arms can be overhead, palms touching. It is a pose of balance and muscle control and strength. With practice, it is almost impossible to wobble. After some weeks, the pose can be altered apparently slightly, when your arms are overhead, by opening the fingers of your touching hands and (this is the crucial bit) looking *through* them to the ceiling. On some mornings, when you have a big day ahead, it feels as if the courage to turn your eyes upwards, to look through the fingers, is more than you can muster. Your wish not to wobble is overwhelming. The fear of being less stable than yesterday is paralysing. You just don't want to try. On these and similar occasions, I invoke the spirit of my Amazonian yoga teacher in the leisure centre of my mining village in The National Forest, ever-generous, who used to say 'Wobbling is just a sign you're working, well done!' Aha, yes, of course.

Feel the fear and do it anyway, as they say; probably 'badly' (a non-yogic term, too judgemental), but do it. Then, in a while, go from there into 'willow', bending from the waist left and right, mimicking the raw material of woven baskets. Or, obviously, skirt round yoga completely if it's not your thing. Perhaps just ask what you should be looking towards, through your metaphorical fingers – do you dare to look and are you okay with wobbling as a form of work?

Chapter 1

Going for a chief executive role: should you, and how?

Only a relatively small proportion of the working population will ever become the chief executive or managing director ('Do the math'). Whilst naming and addressing the myriad reasons why so many people don't achieve their potential and have life chances denied them remains a challenge in our century, it is misleading to say that self-belief is all it takes to get us all to the organisational or political 'top', wherever that is. It can't happen, numerically. But thankfully being the boss is not a role suited to everyone and many wise and talented people will finish their careers very much happier and productive for having been well-placed in a supporting or technical role. Briefly drawing on my experience as a chair, of a charity, I had an extremely supportive vice chair, who picked up the internal processes in a very thorough and dependable way; it was so helpful to have her alongside me. Yet when the question of who would be the next chair came up, she was emphatic that it was not her. Such self-knowledge and lack of fixation on the leadership role are really admirable and helpful. Moreover, you can rightly decline one form of leadership role at a particular time but be excellent for another one; I could see from what I knew of her working life that she was capable of being a very effective chief executive and it was very much a question of timing about which role worked for her. I have also worked as chair and as a mentor with people in an interim chief executive role and encouraged them to imagine themselves in that role permanently, because I believed it was, potentially, the right time and place for them to go for it.

So, whilst is it not for everyone and has to be the right moment, like anything (moving house, becoming vegan, starting to wear brogues), if it occurs to you more than once it may have some traction. Why does the thought pop up again? Perhaps imagining yourself as a chief executive does not seem as daunting and surreal as it did a year or two ago. Perhaps you've now seen a few chief executives in action, and realise that there are many ways to 'skin a cat', the most important thing being to retain your personality and approach, adding to it round the edges and adjusting it depending on the organisation.

I once interviewed someone for their first chief executive role and wondered why she seemed to be under-selling himself. It emerged that her current chief executive was what she called 'charismatic', whereas she saw herself as 'focused' and a 'bit of a geek'. Actually, what our organisation wanted WAS a lot of focus and there was plenty of evidence that she led people well. All she needed to do was release herself from that particular image of a chief executive (a charming networker who possibly did not know one end of a spreadsheet from another), which was not at all what we wanted.

Perhaps, too, whilst you are not exactly coasting in your current senior management role, the challenges are becoming tedious, repetitive hills rather than mountains that get the adrenalin going; if you are perfectly honest you are on the verge of being just a bit bored. Usually this manifests itself in taking a little less care to get the most out of every task. It may be leading you to invest in little projects which meet some of your interests, but which aren't really core. Or you might be beginning to make a few slips in managing relationships because your attentiveness is waning.

If you recognise any of this, or your eyes just keep straying towards chief executive jobs, then remember that, for all that I have criticised those, often the super-fortunate, who say that everyone can rise to 'the top', you have a duty to yourself and to others to take a leadership role if you are likely to be good for it. I write as a US Presidential election comes to its conclusion with worryingly low levels of trust and confidence in the two contenders. There is so much that matters greatly which we cannot change. But, at the wide and deep non-Presidential level, organisations of every size can do great things and they desperately need good – and diverse – leaders.

By this stage in your career, in all likelihood you will have had the opportunity for some personality profiling (such as Myers Briggs and its successors, such as DISC) and if you haven't, I would encourage you to do it. It is possible to do them online for free, or you can spend more and have personal feedback. You need to be aware when using these frameworks that our behaviour at work has often developed in a sophisticated way, so that it is distinct from how we are at home, for example in how much we plan in detail. You need to try to get to your inherent preferences even if you they are not, for good reasons, entirely recognisable at work. Such profiling may then usefully confirm what you already instinctively knew around key areas, such as whether you get more energy from other people or from solitary situations, how intuitive you are, how directive, how good at seeing the big picture, how comfortable being tough where necessary, or in the limelight.

The danger of these profiles is that they encourage you to say 'I'm the kind of person who naturally...' without adding 'but I can and often also do x and I realise I need to do that often'. Justifying putting yourself or others into behavioural boxes is the worst way to use these frameworks. Successful people are deploying a whole range of approaches and working in from any inherent extremes that show in their scores. Very successful people learn to do this without undue fatigue and stress. (And they have had practice; from the time we first sat round a meal table as an infant our social and cognitive personality is being shaped and developed).

So if, for example, your personality profile shows your basic, core preferences to be solitude, a lack of organisational constraints, high levels of detail and endless time to cogitate, then you may find the chief executive role stretching you beyond your base position, but this should not stop you from going for it. If you have that kind of profile (or something not too far from it) and you are already happy in a senior role, leading a team, then you've done brilliantly, working around and adding to your 'gut' preferences and patterns. You are probably much appreciated as a leader for your blend of depth and focus, along with a necessary attention to the wider world. This kind of personality contrasts with the 'big picture', and more extroverted caricature of a typical chief executive; it is said, with some truth, that a more naturally extroverted person finds a leadership role less inherently tiring than a more introverted one, but she or he may need to keep focussed on detail when it counts. The key point here is that the best chief executives flex not only their communication styles but their professional and even personal characteristics and skills, often over fairly extended periods, as the organisational cycle progresses and needs different things. Someone prone to ruminating on success and failure can learn to distract themselves from spending their evenings thinking about work. The person who is inherently bored by accounts can learn enough to read them at the right level of detail for them, when they need to. One exciting thing about leadership at a senior level is that it invites us to stretch ourselves fairly deeply and this is useful for all of life's change points.

By way of demonstrating that there is not one personality type for a chief executive, we could take a lesson from the world of ecology, botany and forestry. This sector tends to attract people who like an element of solitude, a certain timelessness (change being measured in generations and millennia, not financial years) and who prefer not to spend too many hours on abstract reports and systems. They are never so happy as when they are surveying metre squares for species diversity, or pruning trees with an eye to the wood in a century's time. These great qualities of detail and patience risk leaving the sector rather short on corporate leaders who are good at engaging in the hurly-burly, for example defending our precious ecosystems with or against developers and the myriad competing political priorities; it is worth asking why the natural environment struggles ultimately to get the political priority it deserves. Forestry is an interesting example of how personality shapes a sector and then, potentially, the landscape and ecosystems of a nation, depending on the range of skills within the field.

However, two things are happening in the world of forestry. Technically able foresters, steeped in their discipline and reflective by nature, have expanded their skills and become sectoral leaders, rubbing up against people with very different motivations. They often do very well in the multidisciplinary mix we need to build and maintain healthy and balanced urban and rural areas. 'Worldly-wise' operators from other sectors come to respect these people with an eye for the long-term and a deep understanding of the marks which humans make on the earth for future generations. Another way of saying this is that some of the most memorable managers' first instincts were not 'managerial'; they first had technical expertise and lasting passion – and then built on that expertise and passion so that they could do the realpolitik. Secondly, leaders who are naturally multi-disciplinarians and generalists have found a niche in the forestry world and I would count myself as one of these. We bring an instinctual sense of wider interests and have an interesting and rewarding time, always learning from the specialists.

Assuming that you can imagine becoming a chief executive, whether you move one more time before going for a chief executive job, either into another non-chief executive role, either with a bigger team or in another setting, is an important decision. I started working full-time fairly late (aged 30), having had children, done a part-time PhD and learnt a lot through volunteering. I was without a formal professional qualification. I have not had the advantage of working up and through a defined profession, or in bigger organisations. Had I had this kind of background, I might well have 'tacked', (ie moved across departments or into other organisations at relatively similar levels), in quite a deliberate way, assuming I was wanted, in order to gather insights and experience. I did not have this opportunity and have probably had a narrower band of experience as a result.

So, if you have time on your side, think not what chief executive role you could possibly get now, but what your ideal one could be and what would make you the rounded leader you would need to be to succeed in that role. Such an approach may dictate you find relevant experience in a related field at a level similar to where you are now, as an intermediate step. Alternatively, you might be able to move diagonally into a chief executive role in a slightly smaller organisation with a related mission from where you are now. Finally, someone in my family seems to progress rather successfully by covering maternity leaves, as a promotion. If you are good enough, you may well be retained at the end of each one or you can then apply at that level for a permanent role elsewhere.

Whatever you decide to do tactically, if you are fairly sure that you are not fulfilled at your current management level, do not entertain any thought that the demand of the next move is beyond you, or that you will never have your life back. Remind yourself of your track record to date and that each step seems demanding before you take it, but becomes well within your capabilities. The biggest career challenge I felt at the time was when I began taking breakdown telephone calls for the Automobile Association, leaving two babies in the capable hands of their father, for four hours a day. We all survived fine. The hurdles, as you look back at them, are really not so great and this applies all the way through.

It is natural to wonder whether by becoming the head of an

organisation you will have no life of your own, might possibly no longer recognise yourself, become hateful to your children, or otherwise spoil things. Send those thoughts fleeing. Believe that you will not ruin your life by having the weight of being the boss on your shoulders. No job on earth *actually* deserves all your waking hours for an extended period, unless perhaps you are saving lives in a disaster situation where there is no other person to relieve you. Even there, you could never save every life and you would need to come home some time and regroup. To believe your role is so important that it is worth the sacrifice of your health and happiness and those of the people around you is a form of hubris, albeit one so often found dancing around notions of service that it has become, for some generously-hearted (or not so humble) people an accepted truism. It is not true. The one responsibility you have on earth is to yourself and your well-being. All being well, one day you will be old. It is then that your inner reserves are tested, more than at any other time, and techniques of caring for yourself, acceptance of our limited contributions and finding contentment whatever, need to be laid down in youth and middle age.

It is a sign of the most effective leaders that they take control of the balance between work and the rest of life, and I say more about this in Chapter 11 on staying well and happy in the job. It *is* possible. If you suspect that there is something dysfunctional in the organisation looking for a chief executive, making martyrs of its employees, check this out and decide that if you take the job this is one of the things you will change. If you are prepared to go into a stretched public services or a not-for-profit picking up the pieces for very vulnerable people, where, frankly, it might be hard to remove the level of demand, then all credit to you; it will be a central part of your tenure to see what you can do to relieve pressure on colleagues. But please promise yourself not to stay too long if you are experiencing chronic stress because you can't change the fundamentals. You are not responsible for everything and there may be somewhere else where you can do as much good at lower personal cost.

A close friend was recently being seriously schmoozed for a new job, in this case working to the chief executive, in a role offering more money, a good job title (looking to future moves) and based in a suitably characterful central London location. What was there not to like? Nothing except that the head honcho slept poorly, had bad, stress-related eye infections, and was permanently worried about the cash flow. My friend declined the role – wishing him well – because he didn't want to sweat to stabilise things and still find that the head guy wasn't able to manage himself.

I am sometimes asked whether it is dangerous to choose a role for sentimental or personal reasons, for example because you have always supported the cause, or you used to be involved in or belong to the organisation. Clearly if you have unfinished business from much earlier involvement with the organisation, resulting in a very impassioned but possibly dated view about how the cause should be promulgated, or inappropriate skills despite your emotional connection to the place, then you may be heading for problems. But if you have a sensitivity to the cause, knowledge of the culture and some good networks, you may be very well placed. Robert, the head of an Oxford college, said that he had not been interested in one particular college when approached, because he had no connection with it, whereas he had been an undergraduate at the college to which he said 'Yes'. That seemed to make it worthwhile. But it was not primarily an emotional decision on either side: his academic qualifications and other experience were impeccable too. Another person might have taken precisely the opposite approach, being drawn to places where there was no personal link. Just be aware when applying for a job that saying for example that you've 'fallen in love with Africa' and want to do more for the continent can actually undermine you at interview if you don't quickly add the relevance of your skills. But do not be too icy either and remember to allude to why your heart as well as your mind is drawn to the role. This is relevant for resilience in the tough periods.

Once you know that your next role will, you hope, be that of a chief executive, and assuming it is not thrust immediately upon you in imperfect circumstances, take every opportunity while still in your current post for projects or responsibilities which echo the chief executive role. Without being only tactical, if you have not had such organisational tasks to date, any project with 'risk', 'budget', 'corporate', 'change' or 'strategy' in its title will do you no harm. You need to be able to show this kind of corporate role on your cv and, perhaps more importantly, develop the habit of thinking on behalf of the whole organisation, not only your division or area.

Whilst you are not yet a chief executive, your cv needs to look as if you are pretty much there already. When I am recruiting for a chief executive I will spend two minutes maximum, often less, at the outset scanning the cv. I am looking for:

- boring things, like well laid-out contact details. This tells me the candidate understands the recruitment process, in which various people may need those easily to hand at any point. Everyone should understand this, at whatever level, and if an aspiring chief executive does not, it is a bad sign.

- a succinct and compelling paragraph at the top of the page about experience, skills and passions, which isn't the same as everyone else's. It shows a rounded chief executive product but with a bias in some kind of direction and with specifics which fit the role. This paragraph is likely to be finessed for each role.

- a thematic summary of your core abilities, across roles. What have you consistently been good at through your career? If I take you, what will I get? It might be good to ask people who know you at work about what these are. I was surprised to hear a boss say that she thought my core skill was exceptional stakeholder management. At that stage I didn't really know what this was. After pondering I came to see that it was about people wanting to do business with me and my organisation, because I worked to understand them and collaborate to mutual benefit. You will have similar skills which are rarer than you think. Tease them out.

- a succinct career summary, latest jobs first, which tells me what the main roles have been and what has been achieved. Avoid any hint that you think only at task level: if you say you lead a team, I know this will include performance management; instead put in what your team achieved for the company. Use numbers – turnover, people reached, whatever. Demonstrate growth and change and what the legacy will be or was in your roles. Do not use your industry's success markers (eg quality mark, or another acronym) if they are not well known by the body to which you are applying. Put less detail in summaries of less significant, older roles, but again showing in a nutshell what difference you made. I expect more bullet points against recent jobs and their achievements, as an indicator of impact and complexity.

- summaries of what each organisation did. Don't resort to weblinks, tempting though it is, as these require clicks and those reading your cv will not have time to click.

- qualifications from age 18 upwards, training, publications and voluntary and honorary roles. There is no need to confess – or celebrate – your GSCSEs/O levels at this level.

- your personality and passions (selective!) You may not want to disclose your family life or your musical tastes, but what kinds of things do you invest time in out of work? I say more about the importance of thoughtful disclosure of yourself in the next chapter.

Become multilingual, thinking laterally to express the results of your labours. I remember saying to a coach as I prepared for change that I seemed to have spent a lot of time sorting out the board over the last year and this didn't seem too exciting. 'Ah, great,' he said, 'you are leaving the organisation with appropriate governance arrangements for the long-term!' Indeed I was. Yes, of course.

There is no real prescription on length – it depends on the culture – but your cv must be readable, with white space and utterly without typos or inconsistencies. There is no excuse for any grammatical, spelling or punctuation issues at this level and I have often not shortlisted because of presentation. This is quite justified if one of the chief executive tasks is quick production of accurate documents. Think carefully about your font: Times New Roman is now the equivalent of copperplate, in my view, and too bookish for my worlds, but don't go for a large and childlike alternative.

Once you've done your cv, use it to think laterally about the skills and knowledge you have, asking what kinds of roles you could move sideways into. Now is a good time to get some career coaching if you haven't had it, particularly to garner some new ways of seeing yourself. A lawyer who had also been an academic shared his cv with me. It was fine as a record of two successful careers, listing activities and achievements, but for roles beyond those two worlds he now needed to recast the top paragraph to say high level and transferable things like 'outstanding ability to assimilate complex information under pressure and propose solutions'. He might move into a policy or legal advice role with an NGO for example, or a training role in this field.

Once you know what you are marketing, there are various things you can actually do, to help secure a chief executive role. One is to contact recruitment agencies and get your cv on their systems, but more importantly keep in touch with their lead person for your sector. It is definitely worth doing this, as your name might well come to mind when a role comes in. Remember to sound positive and in control of your career with every communication. You are not begging them to help you find a job but saying that you are making a move and might be able to help them in certain roles, being as specific as possible about your criteria. Keep in touch regularly, perhaps around once a month, by email and an occasional phone call. As you will know by this stage in your career, be courteous and friendly with the less senior staff and be super-poised with them too because the leads could come from different people. Every interaction reveals aspects of you and may get be commented on.

However (and I can only speak from my experience), whilst contacts with recruitment agencies are probably necessary and are certainly a good idea, hope too much in them and you may be disappointed; you need to stay proactive on your own behalf. A second means to find your chief executive job is to identify your preferred organisations, connect with them via social media (including LinkedIn) and check out who you already know there. If you can, go and chat to someone, preferably the chief executive, just saying that you're interested in their work and what their future plans are. Again, you may be contacted when a job comes up and certainly you will have impressed them with interest and being proactive. Bear in mind that agencies find candidates by ringing chief executives and others for ideas, and your name may well come up in respect of a job elsewhere, especially if you have actually met and talked with someone recently. Chance favours the prepared mind, they say. Equally, networking, listening, and chatting prepares your mind for change, which may then come from any quarter.

A third means to find get a chief executive role is of course to reply to an advertisement. Recruitment agencies tend to poo-poo the advertising process but some organisations (either with a big enough HR department to handle it or no budget at all to use an agency) only advertise, and of course find people as a result. If you do respond directly to an advert which has been placed through a recruitment agency, do schmooze them, as they may be more motivated to push the candidates they have found through their search, to the client. I have just recruited a chief executive who found the post directly, rather than through the headhunters whom we were paying; inevitably it's tempting to think we could have saved some thousands of pounds, but there you are.

A fourth means to get the role is, of course, to be approached by the agency which is handling a post. Be aware that their first task is to present a not-embarrassingly-short initial list to the client, so don't be so flattered that you spend ages working on an application which is completely out of your reach. It's not just a game of numbers for an agency, but it will have pitched to the recruiting client on the basis of incredible knowledge of the sector which will generate, say, twenty 'credible' names. Such uber-confidence is then sometimes compounded by clients wanting a diverse long-list, to foster their own belief in themselves as interesting to a wide audience. I was once asked if I would consider a chief executive role in a prestigious London Borough. At 48, I'd never worked directly in local government and I would have been utterly at sea. But the client had said they did not want 'the usual suspects'. I would have been unusual, certainly. On the other side of the fence, when I have been recruiting as a chair, savvy candidates contacted by the agency have rung me up to check whether they really did have a chance, given the specification. It's unpleasant closing down a potential career move for someone, but I will always be honest if we already have six people much closer to the core requirements; in all probability it's the agency casting about and not being rigorous enough.

Once you have established that the role might be suitable, be confident in finding out about it from any source. Do not rely just on the recruitment agency as, whilst you might imagine their key strength is to understand one role compared with another, they may or may not be the sharpest tools in the shed in precisely this territory. This fact is rather baffling, but seems to be borne out by many people's experience. If you can talk to the current chief executive, do, and ask around the role without being critical or interrogatory. Remember to flatter: 'From what I've seen it looks to be a very exciting time for organisation X' (even if this is code for a disaster on the horizon). At all times assume that anything you say may get into the recruitment process informally or formally, as the chair, faced with quite a daunting responsibility, will look for corroborating evidence from a wide range of sources and is likely to ask for views from the current chief executive.

On the mechanics of applying, this varies with the role and what follows is general guidance. At this level, any covering letter should indeed look like a letter, albeit probably electronic, and not reside in the body of an email. (Your email, if you are not using an entirely online system, need only say a polite and warm version of 'Please find attached…'). Firstly, even or especially at this level, the letter clearly needs to cover whatever you have been asked to address and whilst it might sound pedestrian, don't dismiss laying it out against the criteria for the role (which could be both the job and person specification). I expect you've been involved in recruitment and felt the relief when a candidate helps you check that he or she has covered the criteria. As per the cv, include examples, numbers and a focus on what impact you made. Break it up, edit it down, but cover the ground. It does not matter if it repeats information in your cv, but do make it count against the specification for the new role. Do not breach any specified length, at all; it looks as if you can't control yourself even in small things. If the job and person specification are pretty dreadful, with 30 bullet points each, you will show leadership by grouping and prioritising them and giving your own group headings such as 'strategy and budgeting' or 'people skills'. Don't be afraid to be more sophisticated than at a lower level, but cover the ground and perhaps say why you're laying it out as you are (very briefly).

The second thing the letter needs to do is to convey enough of your motivation, personality and approach to make people warm to you and begin to sense your appropriateness for the role. In the end, decisions on senior appointments are often made between candidates with not dissimilar similar skills and experience and it is perceived cultural fit and ease of working with a particular candidate that counts in the end. Self-knowledge about your strengths is good to read. This takes a bit of confidence and it is worth re-reading the application and asking someone else to, so that the tone and emphasis seems right. (One difference between doing an application at this level and at less senior ones is the amount of time, specifically elapsed time, it will take. Start it early, do a number of iterations, don't stress and try to show it to someone else whose views you trust. This means a bit of time from start to finish).

Thirdly, and this is particularly vital for the chief executive role, you need to show your understanding of the organisation and your respect and enthusiasm for it. Few candidates say enough about the role and the organisation, either in their applications or at interview. They talk too much about themselves. The panel needs to be flattered and definitely needs to see that you have picked up the main strategic picture. There is so much online that you should be able to sound as if you have grasped quite a bit about the operation. Sacrifice stories of your glorious professional story for space to demonstrate how the organisation needs you.

So, under a section around management style, you might quite accurately say 'I am an effective manager who has used this to drive change X in my current role'. This is fine, but more powerful would be 'I have the capacity to flex my management style as needed, including being directive when required. I showed this in securing the future of X (current organisation), and, given the dispersed senior teams at Y (new organisation) and the urgent need to grow Y's services, shown in the annual report, I would manage the senior team dynamically and against targets, to secure the figures contained in the strategy'.

I would always end a covering letter with my best wishes for the organisation and the recruitment process. It cannot be stated too strongly, but you must come over as poised, chief executive material at every moment, whether it's a short email about arrangements, what you wear to first interviews with the agency, or even how you receive feedback if you were not successful. You need to sound in control of your feelings, your diary, your application, your career and any questions. The default demeanour throughout needs to be relaxed positivity, with flashes of enquiry, reflection and challenge – and real smiles.

If you are long-listed, keep finding out about the organisation and interrogate again how your profile can be shown to match its needs. You are trying to anticipate any probing around this potential match that the agency may undertake. Your cv may have been light on reorganisations for example, just because this hasn't been needed in your roles, but the job you're going for may need this restructuring. Be prepared to show how you have made tough management decisions and how you know that you are capable of this.

Again, even if 'just' meeting the agency, do focus on how you want to present yourself: clothes, bag and so on. This may be informal, if you judge that right for the organisation, but make it a conscious choice. Go with prepared questions and be on the front foot; be the well-prepared chief executive in fact. But at the same time, one of the main things they are doing is trying to get a sense of the person, so, as ever, and this is a constant theme of this book, be you and don't be afraid to reveal what makes you tick. In the end they might not want what they see, but that's better than ending up in the wrong place for you.

If you make the shortlist, you are usually in a position to ask to meet the current chief executive and/or speak with the chair, and do request this if you'd value it and it is not automatically part of the process – or has been banned! You might also meet with the team at this point, with a visit arranged to the office as part of the process. Whatever is said about the purpose of this (for example, 'your opportunity to see the set up'), the organisation would be very foolish to put on such a day and not make assessments from it. I have found it very useful in chairing a final panel to have garnered the views of team members from these days. The quality of your questions as a candidate, your ability to make people feel comfortable in a group conversation and even your face in repose may get reported back. Make it count. I received feedback as chair of a panel that the senior management team felt one candidate was aggressive in her questioning, but the trustees had a much better impression. We were nervous about appointing someone who seemed to use the people she would line manage mostly as mines of information, which she then used courteously with trustees.

If you avoid these mishaps, then you may get to final interview, facing a panel whose views are likely to be helpfully informed already by a whole range of data. There is much written about interviews which I will not repeat, but specifically for a chief executive interview, here are some pointers.

- Check again whether there is anything that might be giving rise to questions in your application, for example that you've moved about a lot or not very much at all, or have left somewhere without a job. Often these kinds of things are the making of you and are pluses, but you need to be able to tell the story.

- Whilst I keep labouring the point that you must stay 'in role' as a credible chief executive, don't be seen to take managerial control of this particular room. As you walk in, deal with nothing except yourself and simply say you are glad to have the opportunity. It's not the time to tut and move the water jug or ask how it's going for the panel, in the spirit of enabling conversation (generally a good chief executive attribute, but not great here). If you have been doing consultancy, your default might have become to ask questions and panels do not like to be interrogated, except by invitation. So, focus on saying how you will serve the organisation's needs in their widest sense. For a chief executive, understanding the status quo, partly by asking questions, is fine, but it is only reaching basecamp. You have to be showing solutions from the word go, even if they are not quite correct.

- Help the panel in deciding if you are the right match. Don't just go on about yourself, but, as per your application, show that you understand what the organisation needs now and how you can help. Self-knowledge, knowledge of the organisation and the relationship between your understanding of yourself and the organisation; this is the key territory. Remember that the panel are not the people running the place on a day-to-day basis and they may even not have a great deal more handle on the strategic issues than you have, after your research. So do show you have some kind of interpretation of these and where you would take the organisation. Even if it's not quite right, it shows the level you're operating at.

- You must answer every question. A frontrunner I once interviewed lost the job because he said he did not have enough information for a question on the financial risks facing the organisation. There will be a finance question, possibly around risk. If you are not a finance specialist, get someone to read the accounts with you in advance and give you the headlines. Then retain the information and answer the question. This is a key chief executive skill. Opting out of a key aspect of the operation will lose you the job.

- You will almost certainly be asked a question on managing people, in some form. They will want to know if you can 'flex' your style, being prepared to be tough or collaborative as needed. Have examples ready. It might be the moment for self-deprecation but don't end your remarks on a negative about yourself. Here's an answer showing self-knowledge and the ability to flex styles: 'My natural style is probably around coaching and encouragement. At the same time I guess I can come over as a bit of a taskmaster at points – I can certainly be tough, but I hope my colleagues see this happens around urgent and agreed business needs at that time, not on my whims. Then the coaching and encouragement side can reappear'. Or indeed the reverse, if that is true and what is needed.

- There are some key concepts in the role of chief executive you need to show you live and breathe. I would hope you have engaged with them enough in your current role to do this convincingly; the main ones are risk, strategy, resources, key performance measures and long-term viability. Even if you are not asked about them explicitly, make sure you demonstrate your comfort around these areas. Weave them into your responses in and make them concrete. How have you made sure a team or company has stayed on track, negotiated risk and planned for an uncertain future? I once interviewed four people in a day and heard a lot from nearly all of them about softer concepts such as 'alignment of perspectives' and accountability; these do matter in delivering good process, and are worth mentioning, but you want to be the level above this slightly abstract language, giving good examples with confidence in your voice. The person who was offered the job identified a risk around long-term delivery, and explained how he would focus on it.

- If you are ever asked a question about where you are on a scale, for example from tyrant to counsellor, never duck out of putting yourself somewhere – and then show how you flex depending on need. If you can, show how you learnt to adapt your preferred way of working. A good moment for wry humour and, again, mild self-deprecation that doesn't go as far as showing low self-esteem...

- At the interview or at any other point in the recruitment, expect more personal probing than you might face at a lower level, possibly around your circumstances and certainly about you as a person and leader. An intelligent recruitment process at this level accepts that a successful leader needs the background context and inner resources to handle the stress of the job. The interview should be structured to leave quite a bit of time for personalised questions, if they have not been asked before. In my view asking exactly the same of everyone is pointless and has nothing to do with equality of opportunity.

- Expect a tougher experience than you might have had at interview up to now but do not interpret a hard interrogation as a negative sign. Mostly it shows that the panel is seriously interested in you and wants to see if you are good under pressure. I interviewed someone whose psychometric assessment had told us that she might be much less assured if we took her away from prepared territory and we should throw some curveballs. We interrupted her presentation to test this, but it wasn't because it was particularly weak. Unfortunately she did not deal with the curveballs particularly well. The skill of keeping a part of you on the riverbank looking in on events and thinking tactically, whilst also being entirely present, is one to cultivate for the future, as a chief executive.

- When you get up and walk out, the panel will notice a tired rucksack or a crumpled pack of papers. If you think this goes inseparably with you and probably with the organisation, fine, but on the whole, neat and minimalist work rather better in the interview room. Don't dress so sharply however that you look as if you have scared yourself! A chief executive should look comfortable and I say more about clothes and self in the next chapter.

- I can only speak for myself, but I do not find it helpful for a candidate to provide additional material such as a portfolio of other work, to read during or after the interview. This will not be a decider, is potentially distracting and it communicates an air of under-confidence. Make your presentation count in the interview. I also think it unhelpful to send an email afterwards saying how much you enjoyed meeting the panel and/or offering more information. If the panel needs to be in touch with you, it will be and its main challenge at that point is finding the time to discuss the results together, not aided by further emails. Other people however like this. I would just say that for me, less is more.

- Close the interview with poise, however it has felt, because you may have done very well indeed in a deliberately tough session and you mustn't throw it away. If you haven't made it for this role, a member of that same panel may hear about a job you are well suited for, the week after the interview.

- Remaining 'in role' as the perfect candidate applies to the bitter end. I have just given feedback to a candidate who already knew she had not been successful, whose panel I had chaired. I didn't have to do this, but wanted to offer it as a courtesy, in addition to what candidates were given from the agency. Having accepted the offer, the person was grumpy and uncommunicative on the phone, as if the call had been imposed. I absolutely would not now recommend her for a chief executive role if an agency asked for names, because I could not be sure that she would be positive and poised in defeat.

But of course it is tough not to succeed and really tough to keep going when you've had a string of unsuccessful interviews. Think of it as your training. Above all keep going at it; it is rare not to make a successful move in the end. Make sure you keep enjoying other bits of life as best you can and make the most of opportunities in your current role so that there is some momentum there if possible. Take on a new role out of work. Go to some classes not at all related to work to prove to yourself that you can still learn. Good luck!

Chapter 2

Arriving: Imagining a successful departure

On appointment to the role of chief executive, the immediate re-action is, pretty obviously, to be chuffed that you've 'got the job'. During the recruitment process you persuaded the panel that you had the capabilities for this particular role. You were the best person and this is truly quite some achievement. Well played indeed. It's a potent mixture of feelings, including trepidation, with a real overlay of relief and a sense of arrival. But in this chapter I want to say why this way of describing what has, very pleasingly, just happened takes you nowhere in particular; it isn't creative or useful to linger too long on having *acquired* something, however much it feels a little like a moving into a new house. This chapter is about how to capitalise on your situation, not dwell on it.

It's a bit similar to saying 'I've just had a baby'. The phrase is used so commonly that we know what we mean, and there is definitely a noisy object that wasn't there before. But 'having a baby' is not an event about new ownership, like acquiring a house and 'have' is a strange verb for being thrown alongside a creature which we never truly possess. What's just begun is a dynamic relationship between you, in which neither party is static and in which ownership is a comforting, but deluded, concept.

When you 'get' a senior job, especially a chief executive one, what's happened is that at the final selection there was enough of a match for you to begin a series of new relationships; with yourself in that role, with the organisation and with all the people now thrust into this relationship as more or less willing parties. I can't emphasise enough how helpful it is to cast yourself as no more or less than a lead character in the unfolding story of these inter-connected rela-tionships. Like any successful relationship there needs to be a good balance between self-centredness and generosity at their heart. You need to think about the story's ending as it opens, and where you want the players to be at its close, as you begin your no doubt im-pressive improvisation as a key character.

Unlike being a parent, which sits deep in your being till you die (I would say, even for those who face the sorrow of losing their only child), as chief executive, you are being paid to shape the role, get as much good achieved as you can and then leave it at the right moment, with you and your organisation content that a good job's been done. Unlike most relationships you should give time at the beginning to think about how it will end. But unlike a pre-nuptial agreement it is not anticipating things going wrong, but picturing how to steer things so so that they go right. Like fostering, and speaking as a former foster parent who recently spent a lovely couple of hours with our former foster son and his mother, now reunited, there is an aim, a focus, and it is all to the good if it's time limited.

Achieving a good departure depends on planning for succession from the outset, not just in relation to the organisation and staff, but including your needs. Self-centredness is a legitimate starting point; asking yourself exactly what you want to achieve *for yourself*, by being in this role. Others may not need to know much about this, but it's very important that you ask the question of yourself and answer it honestly and comprehensively. The more you ask and answer the question, the more motivated you will be and thus better at the job. To do this requires knowing things about yourself, beyond your immediate wanting a new and challenging job. To a certain extent this applies in all roles, but with the chief executive role there will be an incessant focus on where the *organisation* needs to get to, so it's worth consciously allowing yourself time for your own agenda.

When I was appointed to my most recent role I was, as described above, thrilled to get it. It was a great project and one which which would evolve, change and challenge. But I was also pleased for these *personal* reasons:

- I had the chance to move from a city in which I'd had a full life but from which I was more than ready to move.

- I could try living in a village, which I'd never done before.

- My children quite liked the idea of Mum leading a semi-rural life, but in striking distance of London and their home city.

- On a more mundane, ie financial, basis, as someone who had started full-time work relatively late and might want to have her own, probably precarious, business in the future, I wanted to stay long enough to make some savings and some pension contributions.

My *professional* reasons were:

- I wanted to prove to myself that I could learn about a new area, ie land, forestry and the natural environment more widely.

- Having previously done start-ups, I wanted to prove to myself that I could inherit an existing organisation and add change management to my skillset.

- I wanted to leave the organisation more sustainable than when I inherited it.

Awareness of when these needs had been met would help shape when I might be ready to move on – which would also depend on the needs of the project at that time. I would also be aware of my age, how quickly I would be likely to get bored, my appetite for other roles, and the state of the job market, clearly.

There should be absolutely no embarrassment about articulating to yourself and others, as appropriate, your personal needs going into any job, but in a chief executive role where your contentment and motivation are so important, to do so is vital.

If you ever have time to stand on the riverbank rather than going with the flow, you might enjoy reflecting on the traditional four stages of life in Hinduism. Brahmacharya, the student stage, lasts up to about 25 years old, when one is celibate, building identity, learning and trying new things. Grihastha is the parent/householder/earner stage, a life full of commitments and interdependencies. Vanaprastha is the retired stage when responsibilities can begin to be passed over and an advisory role is adopted. One may withdraw to the forest with grey hair and wrinkles, so long as one's dependents are cared for. Finally comes Sannyasa, the renounced life or the begging ascetic, not dependent on possessions and casting him/herself on the mercy of others. (In Hinduism this stage can be entered at any age after the student or celibate phase). These are fun to ponder and contest; as with all typologies, we will claim we are a unique hybrid and question their cultural and gender-bound assumptions. I find it useful to ask not what 'stage' I'm at – I don't think the Hindu ones do exist for us in a linear or an obvious 21st century way – but rather what emotion is engendered by imagining each stage. I suspect a lot of people in their 40s and 50s long for a bit of student and a bit of hermit as well as the all-consuming daily grind. How can we adjust life in response to the emotional pulls which arise? I discuss 'what next?' further, in the final chapter.

So, as you transition to a new role, at whatever level, it is appropriate to indulge in looking after Number One. Then, as you begin your new role you need to cultivate a counterbalancing clarity about what the organisation needs. These are the kinds of questions you should be asking:

- While you're in post, what are the big boulders to move? What are the likely timescales? Whose view of those boulders will you seek in the early days? Will you record them somewhere, at the outset? Whose views on this are most worth hearing?

- How much stability is the organisation likely to need: what is the minimum length of time for you to be there without it experiencing destabilisation if you go? Forgive me if this sounds pious, but leadership is about service and, major personal calamities aside, it is at the very least a significant choice to up sticks and leave when there is risk to the organisation, or some cycle going on which clearly needs continuity of leadership. You will not know the answer fully as you arrive, but some of the potential risks are probably identifiable.

- How fast is change likely to happen, to the extent that the reasons for your appointment might become outdated? The right chief executive for the phase you have been appointed for may be distinctly not the right one five years later. I return to this in the chapter on departing.

- What's the likely PESTLE (political, economic, social, technological, legal and environmental) context during your time as chief executive?

- Can you encourage openness about this likely timeframe with your chair from the beginning?

Once you start considering these questions, it will be easier to imagine getting the team and structure in place to achieve the likely priorities of your time working together.

Signing your contract is a critical, formal, moment and you should have read it carefully and checked it against the contractual norms for the organisation to be sure that you are not being treated dramatically differently from others. Notice period is important; more than three months is often unhelpful for the departing person and the staff, but is sometimes put in because of the time needed for an appointment. Between confirming the appointment and your first day, you should be pondering the circumstances of your eventual leaving; you'll have less time to think about it once you're into your first year, so do it now. Indulge in a little reverie. Ideally:

- What will your personal life look like then?

- Where will you have been stretched and what have you learned?

- What will have been achieved in the organisation?

- To meet, say, 80% of these personal and organisational goals, what do you need to do?

It is good to write down your answers to these. They seem more legitimate and tangible, particularly in an electronic document where you can revisit, update and comment on them in due course. It seems as if an authoritative friend is looking out for you. But it is also good to talk them through with someone trusted.

In gardening, a plant is 'pot-bound' when it has had too many months or seasons in that particular pot. It's an indicator of garden centres with too much stock and slow turnover. The plant is then difficult to extract from its pot and less likely to establish somewhere else in a larger pot or new ground. Typically, the advice is that you should tease out the roots so they are not all madly circling the contours of the pot like tapeworms. However I read the other day that sometimes it's more effective to take a good serrated bread knife and just shave off the roots vertically, all round the pot, like someone in the chippy attacking a kebab on its spindle.

Effective, but brutal; you don't want to have to do that to yourself or have anyone else do it for you in a few years' time. Be in control at the start, tend your own needs, and be generous to the organisation; picture your departure before you get bound and stuck.

Turning to your arrival, there is much in the leadership literature on the tasks of the initial 100 days and, at the very least, reading some of this before a new job focuses the mind and helps you set your own agenda. Here I want to complement this by looking at the *self* which you are revealing, rather than the tasks you are performing. I would suggest that doing this is a vital part of your private aims for this arrival period: it will speed up acceptance of change by your new colleagues and reduce confusion and inertia.

It's possibly a little alarming to realise how much the echoes of how you arrive in a chief executive role are present much later on. My offsprung are well and truly adults, yet I still recognise the personalities they had as babies. That's explicable and rather lovely, if also surprising. But months or years into a chief executive role, should I really be living the legacy of the personality I presented in a less than thought-out arrival? If not, what would lay down the best foundations in the first three months?

I suspect that I have been towards the more intuitive end of the spectrum in presenting myself to a new team, rather than the conscious, probably here leaning on my fairly well developed ability to read people and my effect on them. However relying on one's strengths unreflectively is the one thing that reveals their holes, and early impressions stick. If you operate intuitively and just let things flow, you could be making life more difficult for yourself in the future, if this means you fail to signal key things about your approach. If the team can't read where you're coming from, or can see aspects of you that really don't fit the organisation, whether that's being the last in the office in the morning, or always the last at night, their confidence in you is reduced, when these things are easy to avoid with some thought. However I am emphatically not saying that you should be constructing an artificial persona; above all you need to be perceived as having integrity, and much of this hinges on consistency of values and personality. You just have to be conscious about how you will build the trust of others in this new person and make decisions of where you compromise on your preferred style of operating. Saying why you are doing as you are doing, to key people (such as your PA) is a good idea. Colleagues' eyebrows may be raised in her direction first.

Practice revealing sufficient of the 'you' which exists beyond work early on, in an appropriate way. A professional contact once said to me that the chief executive of her organisation was leaving after some six years and that people still didn't feel they really knew much about her. The tone of the remark was of mild frustration, perhaps even some sense of rejection; how is it possible to work effectively with someone who has never entrusted you with anything personal? Maintaining what can be intensive work relationships is difficult without some sense of the person beyond work, and the fun and mutual interest which this enables, albeit this has to be managed so that the office doesn't become the local coffee shop.

A confident chief executive is not afraid to disclose what makes them tick and on arrival it is good to have a plan about progressively sharing information about yourself which is not critical for the work but makes people feel they know you. It is acceptable and right to do this in a controlled way for you and in a non-threatening way for others. You will of course disclose some information to everyone together and some in one-to-ones, but it is safest to assume all information might be circulated. This thoughtful self-disclosure invites others to see and indeed judge you as a real person, to find the channels of connection which work for them and which take the relationship beyond merely a set of technical exchanges. By implication, doing this says that you recognise that colleagues too have hinterlands beyond work and you are going to be interested in them as whole people.

We of course all have boundaries around what colleagues know about us and what we want to remain private. If, for example, I have moved to live near my work, I might not want regularly to share the settling in to my new home with colleagues. Home is home. Yet this can be an area of connection with staff; we have all had hassles redecorating a house or wondered if the neighbours are going to be friendly. I thought nothing of the reactions to a string of parcels arriving at the office soon after I arrived, having relocated, with various bits and pieces for my house; but at one point a colleague commented on them and was clearly curious to know what they were, perhaps wishing to see whether I was a lampshade obsessive or into tricky DIY. Looking back, it would have been a way to build my working relationship, to confide the less-than-exciting interiors of a few more packages; this would not really have compromised my privacy, despite my feeling a little self-protective at the time. On the other hand, I would not have wanted each stage of decoration to be witnessed by colleagues. Nor did I want books to be unwrapped in reception; somehow that felt a highly personal bit of me, even if there was nothing remotely controversial in my choice (in my mind, at least...).

What you wear and indeed whether your glamorous (or otherwise) wardrobe evidently matters to you is, of course, one small but visible sign of who you are, your background and your values. You have, fortunately or unfortunately, no choice but to send out signals about your professional persona through your choices of clothing. Clothes are often (if sometimes simplistically) interpreted as an indicator of conformity or risk-taking, for women and for men. They can be seen to reinforce the ethos of an organisation or to undermine it.

In my own case, I realised at the age of 48, driving to work one day in fact, that I'm pretty interested in clothes, which is mildly surprising as I am not much of a dresser and, if truth be told, hate the underlying values of most clothes shops and resent spending time and money in them. So I deliberately, if semi-consciously, reduce my choice and the time spent looking, by buying a lot of my clothes second hand: I'm small and tend to have decent pickings; the shops are similarly small, and friendly, and I have no option to follow high fashion, but can choose good labels. I love inheriting old shoes from my friend Juliet in her 90s or a dress left out on the 'free to all' table in my sister's flats. I am aware that I have therefore perhaps not the most coherent wardrobe – and not because I am buying the most memorable new one-off creations. This means that I need to backstop my wardrobe with the few basic items for more conventional occasions and try not to slide too far towards the grungy, lest

I be thought too other-worldly or, worse, a middle-aged hippy who couldn't run a business.

That's me and clothes; the point is to know on arrival that you will be communicating something, even by not altering your style at all, and you should be aware of it. The same will be so of what you eat at lunchtimes, the hours you keep, the amount of time you spend with certain people and your communications style from day one (such as the proportion of questions to statements in your conversations). Do you want or need to change anything from your last role, for your well-being or that of the organisation? Now is the time.

If you know the style and background of your predecessor you may find small ways to change things to suit you, whilst quietly asserting your distinctiveness from that person, but take care. One of my predecessors liked big chairs and a large office, which I did not feel was appropriate for me. However, I soon experienced the politics of office layout, which will be familiar to many readers. A solution proposed vigorously by a senior colleague did not seem a bad idea to me, but I soon realised that moving furniture was held to be the domain of another colleague, who seemed quietly unsurprised when rather impromptu efforts didn't quite work out. I learnt to kerb my tendency to respond to initiative, at the expense of checking the organisational issues.

Symbolic issues addressed early on can be useful. A prison governor in a major city whom I knew told me that on arrival he faced issues of prisoner suicides and a staff culture that needed radical change. One apparently trivial thing he did, which seemed peripheral to these enormous problems, was to come down hard on anyone who dropped litter on the exercise yard. His message was that this was a place in which everyone should have some pride, a grim environment but not one to be made worse by rubbish. He also, of course, carried on longer-term work tackling the apparently much greater issue of suicides and cultural change, supported by every opportunity to convey shared responsibility. In my early weeks in one role, I took a leaf out of his book and chose to remind colleagues not to charge home phones at work on the company's electricity; the issue was not business-critical but I wanted to communicate that we were going to up our professionalism so that we could never be accused of being in a time warp – and also signal that I would notice such things. I was not going to be an entirely outward-facing chief executive.

However if you do select some symbolic issues to tackle, you need also to take the opportunity to communicate your underlying point, not just the minor manifestation of it, otherwise a message about phone use may seem merely critical and mistrusting of colleagues. I remember overhearing one colleague saying to another as we left an early meeting, 'And where did that come from?' relating to one of my 'small causes'; I should have preceded and followed such a specific request with a statement about the wider direction of travel and what this was going to require of us, in terms of any shifts in how we worked. I should have sought out other issues which would have illustrated the same point and referenced between them.

It should not take long, perhaps no more than a couple of weeks, before you begin to express your first intentions for the company, in the wider sense, and by then you should be able to do this whilst reminding colleagues of your values and those goals you have which stem from your reading of the status quo. This is not the same as having a fully crafted plan, but it will begin to form a picture in colleagues' minds of where you are coming from and this is reassuring. It is hardly contentious to say something like: 'You know that I think we're doing a great job and we are going to continue to build on all the good professional practice already here. I believe we get things really strong by taking actions step by step – we will need to give attention to the big and the small issues'.

This brings me to the value of early manifestos, of repetition, and of gauging how much direction your colleagues need in the early days. At this point you are gathering information about the culture of the place, doing your own risk assessment and forming your own first year's job plan. You will be selectively meeting external stakeholders or customers and gaining, at some speed, a view on how they see your organisation. You will be fine-tuning your understanding of internal power relationships and identifying which colleagues are likely to be key supporters in the direction of travel which is emerging. All this is fun, invigorating and a little scary, but your early hunches are likely, broadly, to stand you in good stead.

You need to gather up those early impressions within the fabled 100 days, or possibly in more than one bite over those 100 days, and communicate some high-level messages to colleagues, privileging your senior managers with these first, and couching it in terms of checking this out with them, (unless you have a considerable crisis on your hands and know that you have to steamroller some changes through, resistance or not). In this initial phase, saying something like: 'I've been listening to lots of people and learning more about how we work and I'm beginning to form a picture, which I'm sure will develop and shift a bit. But I want to share it with you,' is important. More important still, such communication needs to lead to some request for action by colleagues, even if that is simply something like providing more information on X, or tracking outcomes of certain areas of activity more precisely, or just some people meeting with you one to one. If your early sense is that the business is doing great work but there is a need to sharpen professional practice over the next two years, and that the business will likely have to tighten its belts, then you should say that – and then the request about phones will be contextualised, and make sense.

So here is a flow for, say, the first three months in a new chief executive post:

- *give people a sense of who you are, through your conscious disclosing of relevant aspects of your personality and values, which*

- *allows people to interpret where you are coming from when you play back your early readings, which are expressed in*

- *key headlines, repeated in different ways for different audiences, and which*

- *distil into a manifesto and requests for symbolic or substantive action which*

- *reflect what you have disclosed, prioritised and said from arrival*

- *and bear repetition over the next 100 days.*

Six months into the year, and your colleagues should have a rough idea of the kinds of things you are likely to be saying in team meetings and your job will begin to focus on converting the your messages into changes in what actually happens.

As you transition into the chief executive role, be aware of where the areas of stretch really are for you. There will be quite intangible elements to how these manifest themselves, not the usual quantitative measures of the scale of a job. For many people, the chief executive role may not be a lot bigger on paper than the job you have just left. A lot of people move from a substantial departmental role in a big organisation to the leadership role in a smaller one. I have appointed people to chief executive roles precisely because we needed the kinds of programme skills they had shown in a bigger organisation and because I thought the person would grow into the other needs of a chief executive role. But what else *is* needed?

Tricia, running a national environmental charity, moved into a chief executive role having been a regional manager elsewhere with a budget of £50m. In her new role the budget was £36m so there was no stretch in total amount. Moreover she says, 'I've always been happy to be a "big leader". I guess I occupy the space naturally'. Her reputation is for a very effective blend of warmth and good judgement.

But all the same, despite this comfortable financial level and ease in being a leader, the role felt different and she did experience a real sense of being on new territory. Firstly, working with the board, consciously helping them in their strategic leadership, was different even from working with an advisory board in her former role. She did however meet all board members one to one before she arrived, which was very helpful in knowing their perspectives and beginning to build trust. This is probably possible up to a board of a certain size, where the new chair is relaxed about you having such conversations and where your current employer has no issues about time spent in the new role before departure from the old.

There is more in chapter 8 on working with your chair and trustees but meanwhile it is worth simply saying that the early relationship between the board and a new chief executive has inherent ambiguity until the modus operandi is agreed and you have the opportunity to choreograph it a little. On the one hand, these are your bosses and they may well have been looking forward to asserting their 'bossness' with a new chief executive, whatever the previous relationship has been like. You need to go with this, following in Tricia's footsteps who, by meeting them even before arrival, signalled her willingness to take steers from them. Little asides around board meetings, on the phone at the end of a conversation, or in the car park, will often tell you more, early on, about things the members are fretting about than you'll get later in formal meetings.

Of course, what you are also doing early on is to see where your as yet not fully formed views on priorities coincide with those of board members, what you need to learn from them and where you might want to start shaping their perspectives. Even your questions will show where your early thinking is and demonstrate leadership. All being well, in strategic discussions there will be a good flow between you and them, with neither side posturing about knowing all the critical issues.

More widely than the relationship with the board, in the early days, the fact of the buck stopping with you just does feel different, whatever the previous role. Tricia felt this in her external representation role, with donors, media and partners. Whilst any employee might be expected to be loyal to the organisation and at the appropriate level to advocate for it, as I articulated in the section on what it actually means to be the chief executive, you are required to embody the organisation all the time and in every conversation. These conversations require a kind of suppleness – often moving between small talk, chatting about the other person's agenda and then transmitting accurately both strategic and more operational messages. Good briefings from colleagues are a great help and you should not be embarrassed to say what you want from one, from whoever is the lead person for the meeting. You will likely want something different from your predecessor because tastes vary in briefings. 'I hadn't ever before depended so much on a good briefing, until I was chief executive', Tricia said. 'Fortunately there was already a culture of providing excellent briefings in the organisation, and I have a PA who prepares things and makes sure I have what I need'.

Internally, after a few weeks, if your messages are being heard, trust will be growing and your leadership will be becoming broadly accepted; what you want to achieve will have begun to gain traction with the your team. You will hear themes being repeated, or at least the same questions being asked. This is a sign that your leadership is 'landing' organisationally. However, do not make assumptions that what you said is consistently what is heard, still less what is repeated. Walking the building, Tricia heard herself quoted in a conversation between two members of staff. One was trying to persuade the other of her position on something. Tricia heard her say 'Tricia wants X…'. Tricia herself was at a loss to recognise what it was reported that she wanted and in fact thought it was something she would not say at all, providing the sudden realisation that her perceived position, mis-represented or not, would have great currency in the organisation, a new experience for her. Becoming aware that your name might be used to promote a position that may or may not be your own is a rather unwelcome reminder that no-one will quote a second tier manager to defend their view if they can possibly use the name of the chief executive. Do not be afraid to reiterate your positions and repeat messages at team meetings and ask for feedback through the senior management team about how they are being referred to, out of your earshot.

Having said all this, the arrival is a time of great energy and op-portunity for you and the organisation. Remember that you were appointed because you are clever, personable and thoughtful enough to take people with you. You serve them by saying what you think and what you want from the beginning, refining the messages as you get to understand the people and the issues. Make the most of the first six months. In the next chapter I begin to look at the tools you have for driving your emerging vision; it is definitely not all about confident smiles and *bons mots*.

Chapter 3

Performance Management: A first year's priority

The last chapter showed how a good arrival builds trust and confidence. These are not ends in themselves however, and in the same way that the liver is a charmless but vital regulator of so many functions of the body, performance management is the structural organ which a chief executive must keep in fine fettle in order to get the best out of everyone. Performance management sets out expectations across the entire activity, from recording expenses to meeting strategic goals. It legitimises challenge when what is going on is not good enough and is a vital tool in any change programme. It is not an end of year afterthought but an approach which must be embedded throughout the organisation. A new chief executive may or may not inherit a very effective system but either way it deserves early attention for the critical part it plays. It is a pre-eminent means by which you establish the culture you want and demonstrate your authority. It has its formal appearances in frameworks and assessment systems, annual and half-yearly reviews. Its more significant manifestation is in *every* conversation which ends in a slightly or radically different way of doing a task, communicating with colleagues or taking responsibility for the organisation's success, and you should expect to see these behaviours whatever the pay grade. To achieve this, everyone needs to be able to refer to what collectively we are trying to achieve (growth this year, or consolidation, new markets, or what?) and how we are expected to do that (more conversations with colleagues, fewer?). Performance management starts with and is modelled by the chief executive, in how he or she does their own role and in every interaction with colleagues. You need to be able to say to yourself, in a nutshell, what you are looking for this year, in outcomes and behaviours.

It is the very essence of being a manager to shape the work so that it drives the purpose and strategy of the business. This inevitably, however strong the trust and loyalty within an organisation, involves moments which unsettle, irritate or generate resistance in those you manage. But if done well, performance management, for all its tensions, will be respected and will keep the organisation together:

everyone will know the score about what and how to work and the importance of playing ball. If it is absent, inconsistent, badly implemented or does not command respect, there is an air of uncertainty, a vacuum which may get filled with tactical behaviour, rather than buckling down to achieve shared objectives. I have a dear friend now in his 90s, a former government minister, a farmer and a craftsman. He taught my son to make a pair of bellows, a mere 65 year age gap between them as, heads bowed, they cut old leather rescued from a sofa and hammered in the rivets. The reclaimed leather has a wee tear in it, so it must be said that just a little of the air current is lost. Therefore, alongside their initials and in the style of a timeless motto, they carefully burnished on one of the wooden faces: 'We hope the puff will be enough'. By contrast to this superlative effort and execution, if my friend sees shoddy work – a gate off its hinges, say, only five years since it was hung – he condemns it in a perfunctory manner, declaring 'Idle, idle'. I love the use of the word to denote both the lack of application *and* the ensuing poor results. The work of an organisation without any performance management is idle, in both senses.

Overseeing performance is what all managers are paid for, so you might imagine that this is second nature to people in senior positions. However I have found both for myself, and when mentoring senior managers, that performance management is often an anguished area. Even 'natural' managers have to dig deep into their reserves of courage and fairness to performance manage well, especially at times of change when there can be multiple conversations with colleagues whom one is challenging to go in new directions. In fact, popular and generally effective leaders, who engender the most trust, can have the most difficulty establishing effective performance management. It can tire them more than others because they are engaging empathetically. They may understand the deep personality traits which are likely to make it hard for some people to change their behaviours, and then where do you go, especially if the key tasks for now are actually being done? But this can be achieved by establishing the right tools and objective expectations. It is good to start by focusing on effective performance management by the end of the first year, when you can lay foundations which will make all this easier as you go forward.

Key amongst your de-personalisers, ie business tools, is the system that says what success looks like and in all likelihood you will have participated in this in previous roles. As chief executive you will want to see that it lays out when and how assessments on progress are made, with a clear understanding that this can happen at any time, on an ad hoc basis, but is given more teeth through scheduled reviews, usually at the end and mid points of your year, whenever those are. Most organisations work best with annual job plans that lay out clearly what the employee will do in the year, and how. Make sure these reference the organisational business plan where appropriate. Do not let the plans become a long list of everything the person will do, so that any extra achievement is deemed extraordinary. The framework also needs to lay out expectations of managers, to do reviews, write them up (always a stumbling block – best to ask them to diary reviews *and* write up time), get them moderated if necessary and by when. It is hopeless if review periods drag on when you want to move on to planning the next six months or new year. Planning for the next phase is distinct from, but dependent upon, review.

Central to the chief executive demonstrating objective performance management is your language in giving feedback, when you refer to the business needs of the organisation and communicate this effectively, rather than framing it around your own elation, concern or disappointments. A performance management conversation should not start from a worried 'X, I am really concerned about progress on Y', unless it is clearly understood why Y is so important to the business and you have only recently gone over what needs to be done. Even then, I would argue that being 'really concerned' is too personal. A more effective starting point, having done the normal reconnecting with the person, is 'X, we talked a little while ago about how you/your team are providing a key contribution to Y, which is so important to our plan this year. I want to talk about how this is going, including how the business need is shifting/any changes we need to make to get to this aim faster and more effectively/some new things on the horizon which may create a need to do this differently'.

If you are unlucky enough not to have a performance management framework in the organisation then you need to instigate one quickly on arrival because for sure you need one for the year end or the year to come, depending how close to the year end it is when you arrive. It could be light touch or very thorough, depending on the culture and sector, but without it you lack your main tool for driving progress and managing change. Your first end of year review process is an important marker, the opportunity to show seriousness about performance and fairness in implementing systems, even if you haven't substantially changed the framework itself in the first year. Clearly it is unfair to change any of the criteria for this year's performance awards, unless you arrive near the beginning of the year.

Preparing for the year end reviews should start early. It is helpful to ask of line managers how regularly they are giving feedback and whether there are any ongoing issues they are working at with their reports. Check if and when six month reviews are due to have taken place and whether they have. There should be an expectation that the end of year review grows out of *all* discussions, formal and otherwise, throughout the year. I knew the MD of a large hotel and sports complex who instigated asking line reports how *their* line reports were getting on, on a weekly basis. This was seen as an affront by some of them, but she was adamant she needed to know the issues – and indeed that there was ongoing discussion about performance – so she could drive delivery through her own line reports. The alternative is the unhappy phenomenon of the 'long screwdriver' when the chief executive has to intervene through the layers of the organisation. If this is needed it is a sign of a weak or perhaps resistant link in the management chain, which you haven't dealt with. Is there a need for more precision in communicating what you are looking for in performance management, or more senior management discussion about how to be bold and not just mates? Does someone just need to go because they will never do the tough thing?

No matter what other issues you are dealing with, as soon as you can, review the performance management structure and criteria for any rewards, involving the HR lead if you have one – early on, if they are interested in change, or a little later if they are less so, when you have a sense of what needs changing. Have a look at the personnel files and see how robustly and evenly the existing performance management system has been applied. Take care if the system seems to be either too focused on outcomes in a simplistic way (because there is often an element of luck in hitting the targets and this isn't fair) or too much around just trying hard and being pleasant (because this effort alone won't achieve against business targets).

Although advocates of performance management systems might like to claim objectivity, there are often elements of pragmatism and politics in the awards given (for example, a sense that every few years a competent, successful and hard-working person will deserve a high award even if no one year has been absolutely outstanding). You will need to decide how tolerant you are of this 'flexibility' and indeed whether any financial rewards are given. There is a healthy debate on whether monetary reward assists performance and my view is that it depends on the culture and budgets of the organisation. Board time needs to be given to the performance policy as it is the board which owns it. Get the board to be clear whether there are overarching targets owned collectively so that everyone shares in success or failure on those and make sure that rewards do not reinforce silo working. If it is not monetary reward, how else could success be rewarded? Whatever you decide on rewards, you have a responsibility to identify any line managers who are inflating markings compared with others, which you can do by looking at the files and having a discussion. Ask for a provisional view of gradings in advance of reviews where you have hunches they may end up inflated. In a small organisation you might be able to do this for all your line reports' reviews, which helps a sense of parity. All this ironing out of the approach and making clear your expectations is a really helpful way of putting a marker in the sand in your first year.

Performance management is weak when it is only about *what* gets done, because this can mask *ways* of doing things that help or hinder the wider mission. There has a fair bit of 'bureaucrat bashing' in some quarters in the UK in the early part of the century, so readers may find it surprising that I very much rated working within a performance management framework emanating from Whitehall, while leading an 'arm's length' body of Government. The Civil Service is by no means all red tape and pointless obsession with process. One wouldn't necessarily expect subtlety from a Civil Service framework, but there was a very well crafted inclusion of skills, behaviours and competencies in the main framework, along with how they should manifest at each level. One reason for this might have been that in a large organisation and a political environment people can just want to keep their heads down and get their job done, without making waves. In such environments, the incentives both to take control of your destiny and to look up, sideways and collaboratively from your desk can be few. In that context, behaviours such as working at pace, taking initiative and sharing new ideas need to be articulated and incentivised, as well as getting the desk work done. A performance management framework is a great support in naming and rewarding new behaviour.

I say more about behaviours as core to the business in chapter 6, which focuses on values and culture, but the point is that assessment should become not just whether a target was met, but, for example, whether this was achieved at a cost to colleagues. I have found the idea of 'office citizenship' useful. Who puts the rubbish out, who buys the coffee? It is an example of teambuilding behaviour which could be included formally in a performance framework, not as a hippy afterthought. In a slightly tough year, one member of our administration team instigated fundraising events and socials and we were able to reward this, as a tangible contribution to performance and morale: the chequered tablecloths, bunting and some treats re-motivated the team and this initiative deserved recognition.

I have tended to work in organisations with a big focus on delivery and a scepticism about jargon and abstraction. So I learnt (though in retrospect, too slowly and unevenly), to make all my talk on behaviours as practical as possible, not using much of the abstract language which follows. I would find a way of saying that paying attention to behaviours was critical to the survival and success of the organisation we all wanted to build and give examples such as low levels of communication with colleagues which could lead to fragmentation in the office or lower quality work, because ideas were not shared. If people are working apparently effectively but in silos that is fine until new opportunities or challenges come along that rely on new ways of working; collaboration will need to be the default at that point. Or, if a senior manager has a tendency to point out the negative to junior colleagues, in the guise of being the experienced guru, and never praises, in the long-term this is enervating and toxic; as chief executive, you need the tools to challenge it. One straightforward, depersonalising tool is to say in the performance management framework that a positive coaching style is expected from line managers, core to their pay grade – and they will be judged against this, as well as their teams' completion of tasks.

As ever, in communicating with colleagues, metaphors may help and vehicles are a common choice, for example: a poorly tuned engine may go along but it uses more fuel and makes more noise than a serviced one, irritating passengers and passers-by alike. You can also emphasise the human effects of behaviours: it is tiring to work in an environment where you have to guess what a colleague is doing because their head is buried all the time, whilst it is energising to have a walk suggested at lunchtime by someone with a smile on their face. It is possible and indeed necessary to make language direct and not to talk the language of 'behaviours and competencies', which conjures unfortunate associations with zoological study and schools.

Looking back at my chief executive roles, in retrospect I would have invested more time in the first year to establish how appraisals would be standardised – yet finding ways to be sensitive to all these nuances I have outlined – and would have empowered line managers more clearly to be rigorous, especially those under pressure from their reports not to be challenged and yet still receive a financial reward. To hear the message that the end of year *should* have some uncomfortable discussions is important for line managers, especially in a generally positive and benign management culture. It is good, and fairest on the whole organisation, to do this earlier rather than later.

It is sadly the case that many of us become managers without absorbing the hard truth that your pay increase is mostly for the unpleasant aspects of line management. Sitting with your line managers and giving examples of how to challenge their line reports might be needed, at a very 'word for word' level. Again, looking back, I would have spent more time on this, asking how they could say the unwelcome and coaching them to be able to do so. We would have practised together more often how to say the positive fully, allowing the exchanges to flow for a while, and then making the transition to the challenge: 'One area where I would have liked to have seen something different is…' (Or, of course, you may be in a much more brutal culture, in which case just muscle in and say it – many leaders will be envious of managers operating in that setting, at least in relation to performance management!)

A seasoned manager, embarking on what is euphemistically called 'a difficult conversation', whether in an appraisal or in the course of regular management, will learn to read the signs of how his or her challenges are being received; some colleagues begin to smile more than usual as they silently stack up the reasons why this doesn't sound a good idea, others interrupt when they don't usually do so, some have a change of facial colour. A very few, when being told of shifts that are needed, really can detach themselves emotionally from projects they have been leading and behaviours they've been showing, see the bigger picture, accept the changes suggested and help shape the future, all in the space of half an hour. The most skilled at working with their boss will listen, reflect back and then challenge if they think they should, ultimately securing a way forward that both parties are happy with. Whatever the reaction, try to show you have seen it, understood it and now want to move on.

Job plans for the annual work of each employee, which flow out of appraisals, are a key building block of a successful organisation and the chief executive should have an overview of how the key ones, at least, drive the implementation of strategy. Are they well embedded and could you use them creatively with your colleagues to shift priorities and practice, or are they seen as mechanistic devices by which to carry on year by year without much collective or individual thought? Make it your business to get under the bonnet of these in good time for the first cycle of year-end reviews. Couch this in terms of your learning, for this is what it is. You absolutely do need to know what activity is being taken to drive the strategy and to see if the read across is obvious to you. If, on reading a key job plan, you are struggling to get to the essence of the role, or relate it to the relevant part of the strategic plan, then trust your judgement and say so, preferably early on. Ask if the postholder and her/his line manager believe the job is as clearly described as it might be. It may turn out, for example, that they have inherited it and never quite owned it themselves. It is difficult to underestimate the need for colleagues to be able to articulate their role in the organisation, see its strategic purpose, summarise its main functions and identify the key tasks and responsibilities. It is that fabled moment when John F Kennedy visited NASA in 1961. 'What', he asked of a janitor, 'do you do?' 'Sir,' he said, 'I put people on the moon'. That is the point you want to reach, with the levels below it. Of course, what may be revealed is confusion about strategic direction and then the task is to use job planning to gain strategic clarity with the senior management team, (see below). Don't underestimate how challenging this might be and the time you might need to put in yourself to give examples of what you want.

Chief executives believe, of course, that they are crystal clear in their requests, but if job plans still come back murky, you will have to dive in deeper for now, an investment worth making. This can apply even if you have a strong HR function, particularly in relation to job plans for the people you line manage directly and possibly steering the production of a new template, as there could be vested interests in maintaining the status quo. You may also find yourself moderating between job plans to ensure that there is the same approach and comparable levels of detail. Even in a big large organisation, it may not be appropriate to delegate this entirely to HR; you are the person with overall responsibility for the delivery of the strategy, no-one else, and the coverage, balance and clarity of plans are key to this. Moderating job plans may take some time and diplomacy and getting your senior management team well up to speed. It would be a good indicator of success in relating job plans to the strategy and to one another that they are all posted on a shared drive (minus any training and development areas). Essentially they are not private documents, annual reviews being a different matter.

Your review of the job planning template may throw up some interesting organisational information. You will see a strong delivery culture if plans bristle with well-defined tasks and projects, dates and success criteria against them. As I write, targets are meant to be out of fashion in the public sector, but if your culture is the same, resist the tide, where numbers, dates and other such measures form solid building blocks of organisational success, year on year. They may be necessary and helpful, if not the whole story. Just make sure they are SMART, as HR websites will remind you, and be prepared to send things back which remain too vague. This does not mean everything is numerically assessed; if your PA's role includes effective support to the chair of the board, the best way to know if he/she has done this is simply to check it out with the chair. That is the success criterion and it should be in the plan, with a date.

Less positively, however, such a delivery-focussed job plan may be too busy, too task-orientated and betray a lack of confidence that it is the big things that matter in the end. Space needs to be given for the unexpected; improvisation and taking on extra work during the year is justifiably expected at a lower level than some people believe. For someone at middle or senior management levels, not every deadline for production of board papers should be in there; this is an expectation of the job.

The story of the 'boulders' demonstration by a professor is helpful here. He was encouraging effective study skills in lackadaisical students coming towards the year end. How to make them focus on the important? He produced a bucket on his bench and filled it with large stones. 'Is there space for anything else?' he enquired. Apparently not. He then poured sand all round the stones, increasing the weight of the bucket considerably and illustrating the point that if you put the big things in first, you can fit in others. 'Uhuh', said the students, dimly grasping the point. Then to illustrate it further, the professor poured water into the bucket, which obligingly absorbed it. The smallest particles willingly found yet more space.

The story also implies, reversing the demonstration, you can all too easily fill your bucket with water and have no space for the big things. Place the big, overall aims in there first and prioritise them. When a leader shares this story, colleagues who absorb the point begin to talk about 'moving their boulders', or, conversely, frustrating weeks when they haven't managed to. There should be a clear read-across from the boulders that get mentioned to the job plan. The *most* on-the-ball colleagues rightly also point out that the lesser jobs also need to be done and it is possible to focus on boulders too exclusively; indeed, time spent every so often sorting out the desk and dusting the keyboard, as well as having a good gossip about work and beyond, is well worth it. But the story is still a useful reference point for discussing priorities and time management, which then need to be reflected in the plan.

To summarise, some approaches around performance management in the first year:

- Lead in shaping the rigour and consistency of the performance management systems, in good time for the first full year. If there is a six month point coming up, consider mid-year reviews if they do not usually happen.

- Coach colleagues about fairness and robustness and having difficult conversations if necessary including giving feedback. This latter is best done throughout the year in formal and informal settings.

- Anticipate that performance management will be a significant part of your first year, especially within the senior team. Some will genuinely see their worth in terms of scores and bonuses, fight harder than others for them and reflect this in their teams; others may be motivated very differently. Remember your responsibility is to the whole.

- Review past and likely current markings with senior managers before they do their reviews and say where you think they are more or less generous than the norm. Ensure all those conducting reviews have received the same messages about what excellent, satisfactory and in need of improvement (or whatever you use) are scored.

- Make sure the reviews will be moderated by those above the person who conducts the review (which is the chief executive in the case of reviews done by the senior team) and ensure colleagues know that this is the case, and who signs off final markings. Get involved in the next round of job plans, making them relate clearly to strategy, with clear criteria for scoring. Decide with your chair whether he or she needs to see the reviews you conduct with the senior team. This would be consistent, but might not be welcomed by either the chair or the senior management team, in blurring boundaries and bringing the chair too close to the operational performance of individual officers.

- Make sure job plans include the how as well as the what, to support your performance management around behaviour.

- Help colleagues see the big tasks and reflect them in their job plans.

Finally, performance management applies to, and can be used to guarantee, everything undertaken to protect the integrity and quality of *all* the work *all* the time. There are areas where the most debris, shall we say, would hit the fan if things were not right. This includes the business continuity plan, which could save lives in an emergency, the safeguarding policy, which could stop lives being ruined and the fraud policy, which could save the reputation of the organisation. If you are looking for the corporate points to go in on, to push for robustness, and make the subject of performance management, these should not be ignored. The board will be interested in all these. Make it your business to know whether organisational practice actually bottoms each of these out, with procedures in place and where they sit in job plans. Then use your enquiry to emphasise to colleagues how important integrity and quality are to the survival of the outfit. It is never acceptable to have pieces of paper with nothing behind them and this is a key performance area, alongside every other sphere of activity which drives success.

Chapter 4

Change: doing the groundwork

Until I became a chief executive I had little idea why the phrase 'change management' had such an aura of chill around it. Surely, I thought, this is what managers are all trying to achieve all the time. Indeed, why else would the vast majority of people go to work except to achieve change, whether it is a cleaner hospital ward, teaching a maths GCSE class or completing a construction project? But of course 'change management' is really about leading uncomfortable change, the professional equivalent of moving house because you are forced to, or saying goodbye to a valued relationship to regain life's bigger purpose. It takes its toll as these personal moments do.

The common scenarios for change are the shrinking of funding or the market, or both, a merger or acquisition, or a switch of business emphasis, with the ending of some products and development of others. New technology can disrupt processes and reduce staffing requirements and there may be a strong case for outsourcing parts of the organisation's function (or, reversing that decision!) In my experience the common internal impacts of change are a mood of unsettledness in the office (for everyone, whether they know their role is affected or not), an actual loss of productivity as people wonder more about their job prospects than getting work done, a lot of management time turned inward and the possibility of more conflict and silo working due to people feeling threatened.

Change management is bumpy territory, and will sometimes involve causing pain to people who have done great work, whom you may like and who may feel strongly and negatively about this change. It can share the dynamics of a bereavement and has comparable stages, made all the more complicated by being experienced at different times by people in the same office. It is a time where you will do a lot of talking and listening, and yet feel lonely. It is when you earn your salary and (can) become less fun at home. This chapter and the next go deep into the mechanics and realities of change and, I hope, reassure that this not very enjoyable process is standard fare for the chief executive. It is survivable and often ultimately good for the organisation, even if imposed. You are probably going to do it well enough, even if everybody is unsettled and some people pretty unhappy, for a while. If you do it in a self-aware way it can also strengthen you as a person and a leader, someone who can do the business and practice human decency at the same time. These are inherently valuable – and marketable – traits.

Effective change rests on good communication, generates wise redeployment of resources and results in a better-structured organisation, delivering the very best results that can be achieved in the current environment. Or of course, it might lead to closure, but done with dignity. The rest of this chapter deals practically with how the chief executive lays the foundations for change, before the main decisions about jobs, structure and money (for these are the three essentials) are made.

At the end of a major change process I was relieved and pleased when a senior colleague said to an external person that despite job losses the change had been handled well in our organisation. I asked my colleague why she said that and she said 'You always communicated when you could and you were always straightforward with everyone'. My overall approach during the actual change process, which involved a reduction in staffing and a shrinking of the 'sections' we had had in a relatively small organisation, was essentially simple and built on what I had done on arrival, before any enforced change. I had asked colleagues' views on the key things to preserve, and those that in their opinion needed to change. This gave reassurance that views were welcomed and there was some sense of involvement by all. It also began to normalise the possibility of change. It's helpful to go round the communication circle more than once, feeding back more perspectives and reflections as more conversations have been had, to show that you have been listening. I recognise in myself a tendency to absorb information but not say that I have done so, neglecting to play it back or return to it in discussion, to show that it has been thought through: the chief executive needs to lead from the front in *demonstrating* reflective listening.

Even early conversations with senior managers, quite probably before change is definite, should be used to show that you are not afraid of change (and in fact would be surprised if in all your time as chief executive there is none) and want to know what they think should be different. Be aware however that they may not know how much to say frankly to you at this stage. They may want to give you the heads up on matters that they feel are urgent or unresolved, possibly sensitive, but are unable to be completely open about them, not yet knowing if they can trust you with views that define them against colleagues. So you may receive somewhat opaque messages on what should be different, albeit you are being given detail about what goes on now and there are palpably strong views and feelings in the background. You can find yourself asking: 'What is actually being said here?' and you will have to judge at what point you should ask for a more direct account of the issue. I remember many years ago an impassioned but not entirely clear critique from a manager of the performance management processes, as I arrived in a role. I should have said: 'Sorry, my head's taking in so much at the moment. What exactly do you think should be different, and what are you proposing, then I can bear it in mind when I'm reviewing what we do?' I might or might not have got more clarity but it would have demonstrated that I wanted to know and would reflect on what was brought up. Instead I think I merely grunted and clocked the general rather than specifics.

Whilst conversations with senior management colleagues are particularly important, it is also vital in establishing your change leadership credentials to work beyond your direct line management arrangements and to make contact with the wider staff a norm from early on, openly and yet without taking on a line management role. Without this, you will lose a vital way to influence the wider staff and a channel for feedback about what is really going on. Ensure your reports know about this and do your best for them to accept it happily. Explain how critical it is, for everyone to move forward together, that communication is shared widely and that you understand the wider mood. Emphasise that their senior management views remain particularly important and you will not slip into a line management role with their reports.

In preparing for uncomfortable change, but before it happens, in a small organisation of up to around twenty people it is perfectly possible to speak with all those you will not otherwise see one-to-one, for half an hour, simply asking them to tell you more about their roles, what they like about the organisation and what they would like to see different. In a bigger organisation this clearly isn't possible face to face, but you have other means to gather this information, from online surveys and anonymous questionnaires to focus groups and team meetings and you can be supported by the corporate centre to gather it. In a larger organisation you will need to decide how many people you can speak with and whose perspectives are the most useful; it may not just be the most senior 20 people and if your choice includes a receptionist with a lot of customer interaction this will be a useful signal of your organisational values.

These conversations, even if a little coded or coy, are your opportunity to reinforce that change is likely, to some degree or another, but to reassure that it will be done with care. Face to face chats also allow you to pick up a whole range of other things: whether we share any interests outside work (the briefest of chats in the corridor about such common ground can be especially important at times of difficult change); how much the person feels valued by the organisation; his/her general appetite for change and whether they could be an ally when it happens; how much appetite there is likely to be for promotion in that person; do the eyes say something about a fear or unhappiness which is not yet revealed? And so on.

Turning to the nitty gritty of how you, as chief executive, effect long-term, sustained, systemic change, this will depend on working with and, let's be honest, sometimes against, others. Indeed you may be feeling constrained by the culture, current climate and personalities around you; these are the reasons why change is needed as well as the reasons why it is difficult. Uniformly, in speaking to chief executives, you will hear them exercised by how to manoeuvre in a tight space when, from the outside, they are believed to be where power rests. My chief executive roles have been in relatively small public sector bodies with characteristics of the not for profit and private sectors, where my colleagues have, in general, been very able and committed, and where change needed to work with those talented people, rather than undermining them. In this setting, firing and hiring is often disproportionately destabilising and cumbersome, and is not always a desirable or feasible option. Instead, I have mostly been in the business of finding a whole range of other levers to take my colleagues with me to secure our organisations' futures. The good news is that there are many allies to effect that change.

Firstly, it is rare that you are assessing the need for change by yourself, to the extent that it will come as a surprise to your board. From the moment you saw a job advert or talked with the recruiters, you will have been building a sense of what the issues are, in the views of others. On appointment you will have talked further with your chair and other directors or trustees, who will have spoken more fully now that you have arrived. What has been in code may now be decoded. You will now be listening and teasing out the meaning behind what they are now able to say, checking out what they would like the new chief executive to do, and indeed not do. This should all get processed into your own job plan, with any priorities for change clearly stated, if indeed there are any at this point. Wherever you can, you should make sure that a collaborative approach is agreed between you and the board; this is a corporate project rather than an apparently solo Antarctic trek. History has been kind to Shackleton, but it is worth remembering he depended on a team, which he nearly destroyed, albeit there were brilliant flashes of leadership and the ability to maintain trust in extreme circumstances. You want to avoid leaving some of your party on a hostile shore while the other semi-starved team mates are forced to row through icy waters for rescue; having others working with you is the best way to achieve this.

In a large organisation you are possibly more able to identify within your senior team the 'wise heads', people of good personal and organisational judgement, who 'get' the direction of travel, advise and support you and also provide useful antennae into the organisation. These are the people whom you can trust, personally and professionally. It is a precious thing, for example, to have a Head of HR who will not only help difficult decisions about staffing but also feed you appropriate articles about leadership styles and relate them to an internal issue that needs attention at a time of change. Frances, heading a large national membership organisation, has had that: 'Here's the Harvard Business Review seminal paper on styles – do you need to be more or less affiliative [people-centred] to get this issue sorted?' her Head of HR asked. Gold dust.

Frances, given the scale of her organisation, was also able to put in a highly competent Chief Operating Officer, from within the organisation, to implement much of the practical impact of change. 'In the end, the first point is to be competent, isn't it? And I know she is'. Competence included the *way* this person did the job, which Frances knew she would be happy with. Perhaps more fundamentally it makes such a difference to be able to share the responsibility and not be the only one waking at night worrying about what has to happen next. A shared vision and approach to the necessary change makes the experience much less costly. (Never imagine the boss forgets all the personnel issues over the weekend, when change is happening). If such a sharing is not available, say in a small organisation, you should be generous with yourself if you do find it getting under your skin – and look for support.

When you are in the position of being able to trust colleagues to share the burden of change with you, how they are doing it is what you may receive feedback about from colleagues, possibly fairly late in the day, rather than simply what they are doing. Unfortunately, if you do hear about the 'how', it will most likely be because colleagues implementing changes are alienating people, rather than that they are doing it fine (which tends not to get fed back). To avoid this, a good appointment is someone you've already seen winning people round; it might have been in something small, a systems change, but well executed. Keep skilled change-makers close by. If you lack them in your senior team you will need to shift that, the subject of the next chapter.

Timing is another key part of the mechanics of change. Is it really true, as some management advice suggests, that you have THE window for change soon after arrival and if you don't jump through it you will be struggling to succeed with anything significant? What are the merits of early, decisive change as against more organically growing the good? To use another analogy from my time in forestry, a wise forester may take time with a newly acquired wood to decide what interventions to make. But if you can immediately see that the wood is overcrowded, with no clear paths through it and in a state of neglect, is there a good reason to lose a year in which otherwise its health and your ability to take it forward would be improved?

In terms of whether it is really true that you have to act swiftly, there is no one simple answer. The golden rules of management are regularly tarnished by the ambiguities of daily life and of course a stable transition to new leadership with very little change is sometimes what the organisation needs from a new chief executive. Sometimes, you have been in post for a while before the need for change genuinely emerges further down the line, over time and after a period of consolidation; this can be particularly challenging, as you are trusted by then and probably feel an affinity with the people whom the change is affecting. But looking back at my experience, in my smallest organisations I should have been more ambitious to grow the team in the early days. In another situation, I should perhaps have been more willing to instigate structural change early on, facing up to the disruption and discontent it entails, rather than waiting for external circumstances to propel it. But whatever the scenario, there are some points to be made about the chief executive's leadership, so that change helps you in the longer-term, when the need for change is unassailable.

Firstly, your initial instincts on what seems in need of change will probably have some elements of truth in them, if not the whole truth. These instincts could be about anything, from the software used for financial planning, to how much research and development is being done, to the balance between online and hard copy communications. The best thing is to ask questions, eager for the back stories but prepared to say where you are coming from in the issue. Choose areas where you have the experience and the confidence to come to a view fairly quickly; learn about the other areas.

Secondly, however, although your initial instincts are likely to be useful, leaping in to criticise without enough information is clearly inadvisable. The way people are dealing with things may be very sensible compromises, arrived at through their hard-won experience of the culture and what it enables and discourages. In my own case, I would say I am a quick and relatively accurate reader of what is going on in an organisation, but I have learned that a little knowledge is a dangerous thing, and much the best tack is to use my need to understand more about the issue and to draw key people into shaping the issues. You will not know immediately where all the strengths and weaknesses lie and what is behind, say, an apparent enthusiasm for leaflets rather than online communications. Maybe constant updating of online information and the use of social media, which you would might assume is an efficient way of doing things, would not fit some of your organisation's key audiences and that is why it seems under-developed.

Logically one would expect culture and practice to *serve* the mission of an organisation; they should surely be means to an end. Where this is not the case, and the organisation seems bound by ways of working and style that do not serve its purpose, you will find the answers in its history. You may, for example, wonder why a team when gathered round the table is rather mute, or conversely rather argumentative, and find out as a result of your probing that it is a legacy of earlier days, when there were strong voices who predominated or camps which locked horns regularly. The old protagonists who shaped the team may have moved on and it is as if you are investigating the 'epigenetics' of your organisation. Epigenetics is the way that environmental factors can actually turn off and on the genes within our DNA, thereby substantially altering our traits, even much later down the line and when some other traits might actually help survival and flourishing.

Moreover, in the here and now, teams and individuals are naturally strong in some things and will tend to do more of those things where they feel successful. They then get even better at these, reinforcing and narrowing their expertise, as happens in our personal lives. Samuel Johnson spoke of this in The Rambler, written 1750 – 1752 for social aspirants who needed his sane guidance in conversation and behaviour. (Would that it were that simple these days). 'As any action or posture, long continued, will distort and disfigure the limbs; so the mind likewise is crippled and contracted by perpetual application to the same set of ideas. It is easy to guess the trade of an artisan by his knees, his fingers, or his shoulders: and there are few among men of the more liberal professions, whose minds do not carry the brand of their calling'. He goes on to give a wonderful critique of what I would describe as the impenetrable jargon of each industry or sector and to call on all who aspire to live well to be open to 'common affairs' and the wider professions and world around them.

The same applies in an organisation. The things the team is less good at can get neglected and remain under-developed unless the balance is actively addressed and it is up to the leadership of organisations to make this happen. You need to develop the ability to identify and name cultural myths which have their origins in behavioural comfort zones, for example that for customers to trust us we must answer all queries personally and at length; this might be disguising nervousness about any alternative customer-facing technologies but using up a lot of time in inordinately long personalised letters. As you question practices, you should expect colleagues to be, in part, hiding behind the limits of their skills and preferences to justify what is being prioritised (because we all do this). Shifting this inherent tendency to stay within the safety of what is known to work, our jargon and our daily routines is a niggling, daily task of the chief executive, who must practice also on him or herself.

Thirdly, be confident in acting on any issues which seem no-brainers to you. In her first three months, Tricia, leading an environmental charity, made two operational changes where she could see that implementation of an agreed strategy was not being supported by delivery arrangements. One of her no-brainers was to increase capacity in a key area, which was under-resourced to fulfil its strategic role, and the other strengthened strategic leadership of all income activity. She counts herself fortunate that these two shifts were very clear to her early on (based on her experience and therefore an informed intuition), but which had clearly not been picked up before. These two relatively small changes were means by which she could signal that she wasn't afraid of change, and that beneficial change could happen without a fundamental unpicking of strategy, or triggering a widespread reorganisation. (All the same, she needed to give reassurance to colleagues on these points). I would have liked to observe her do it. I suspect that she listened and overcommunicated about the why and the how, and about the results the change would achieve, and thereby squeezed a whole lot of valuable leadership capital from the process.

So the message of this chapter is that change management should be expected in any chief executive role. It can be signalled and prepared for through small but real changes, properly explained and communicated. You are then ready to do the hard business of restructuring people, money and governance when you need to. This is the subject of the next chapter.

Chapter 5

Change: 'The right trees in the right place' – restructures and governance

Having had conversations and begun to take mostly symbolic and small scale action around activity that needs to change, sooner or later you are likely to need to re-fit people and structures around the overarching business needs. This is going to be messier than it can possibly sound on paper, so let's ease into our consideration of it through a gentle region of the English landscape.

In East Anglia, there are some fine estates growing trees, for timber and for what they provide for the landscape, other businesses and also wildlife. Woods play a major role in the rural economy and way of life. Hornbeam, too dismissively thought of as the poor person's beech, is willing and graceful in this region, and can out-compete oak; conifers can do well, framing the main house and buildings of one estate with strong outlines all year round and providing everyday timber products. The monotony of often flat arable fields is broken up by woods of different scale and size. An expert oak grower and owner of one of these estates was explaining to us foresters how he carefully sources his oak seedlings from strong strains and makes sure that they are planted with care, at the right spacing, so they make good progress. It sounded very precise. Then he surprised a few in the group by saying that actually you only need five out of the original hundred small trees to be any good. The rest can have poorer vigour and shape. Suddenly it all sounded a bit more approximate.

As a forester he was correct; although you would not choose to have substandard stock, prone to disease, and he definitely tried to avoid this, ultimately, when those trees are over 100 years old – a mature wood as most people would understand it – you have very few of the original trees left after waves of thinning. Trees are planted close together for good reason, so that they compete with each other for light and grow straight. But forestry does not work on the basis that every tree has to survive. In fact, it is wasteful to prune the trees of least good form, as they will come out in painless waves of thinning that take place over decades. But what an easy world, compared with managing a team! Here you long for the reverse, at least 95% performing well, close to 100% in a small team with no backstops. Still, there is a similarity between the worlds, if even an estate owner who willingly dispenses with the majority of his trees will take care on selection, placing and nurture. As chief executive, how much more do we need to take care with this, if we can accept a whole lot less 'natural wastage' than a woodsman and – crucially – are dealing with the complexity and potential of the human?

Here I want to say more about recognising skills and talent and, most importantly, moving them around to match business needs (and in this regard the chief executive has a distinct edge in mobility over the forester with his or her trees, as people are more inherently transplantable, if sometimes resistant!) The mantra for foresters is 'the right tree in the right place' but foresters really only have initial planting and removal as their options, whereas you are more of a gardener as a chief executive; often you can move your 'plants' around to see where they thrive best. Sometimes, however, roles and people may need to come out altogether.

For both woodsman and gardener, there is no favourite, general specimen that can be put pride of place in any wood or garden. Personal preference has to be subservient to location, and the purpose of the planting, that is to say the strategy. Neighbouring woods with similar conditions but different owners with very different aims can, legitimately, have a very different look, but choices should be made with reference to overall aims and not whim: one wood might be managed to provide some cash for great grandchildren through timber, long after the current owner has died, and another may be for wildlife for the public to enjoy, or somewhere to bring the grandchildren when you are still alive, to commune with 'nature'. The latter wood may have more colour, more opportunity for scrumping and even, dare I say it, what other foresters would term 'under-management'. (Foresters tend to agree on the benefits of active management of woodlands over centuries, for charcoal, coppice products like walking sticks, or timber, and will itemise the benefits of cycles of open glades for invertebrates. The gloves come off, however, around the operational details of such management).

Forestry is sometimes just a question of growing one species. But there are risks attached to doing so and, as I have been writing this book, Japanese larch (an important commercial crop) has had to be felled in large quantities across western swathes of the British Isles, due to a lethal disease, phytophera ramorum. Mixed woodlands are not commercially as easy to deal with as plantations, because they need more fiddly management, whereas in plantations the same management activity is likely to take place across the site at any given time. But a mixed woodland can be more capable of withstanding disease and responding and adapting to change. A wise chief executive also looks at mix, resilience and capacity for adaptation in the organisation for which he or she is responsible.

Back in the world of human management, and in a similar spirit of making the most of what they had for the long-term, both Geoff, heading production in an automotive plant for a global manufacturer, and Robert, the Head of an Oxbridge college, invested in taking people with them and getting the best out of them. A global automotive company will have a structured process of continuous improvement, based on identifying what could be better. The key skill at Geoff's plant is for every employee to be a 'solution finder' and, at every level, promotion assesses this capacity to find solutions, using real world issues that the employee identifies in the plant. This can be psychologically pretty tough if colleagues bring up your area for improvement, or if your ideas for improvement are not thought viable. Talking to Geoff, who is far removed from any stereotype of a numbers-obsessed manufacturer, it is obvious that the softer skills of encouragement and positivity are key in making this culture of improvement work. The focus is always on processes that generate strong evidence for action, not on people per se, thus depersonalising criticism. Managers are trained to encourage, praise and ask questions, to get people to buy into the process. It is: 'You did well to identify that issue and work through to a solution. Thank you. I wonder if it is worth looking at X, too?' rather than 'It's all very well having made progress on X, but the bigger issue, Y, looks like a basket case!'

In an Oxbridge college context, a federation of individuals, there is no such meta scheme for continuous improvement. Governance is set out and formal, but is also rather dispersed. Power is not cleanly given; personnel issues will and do arise and without the HR department of a bigger organisation, some of these will land with the Head of College. Again, the outside world might be surprised at how much diplomatic energy, time and skill have to be devoted to oiling the wheels of human relationships when the inevitable issues arise.

In a more conventional chief executive role, when you are deploying people and sorting out the structure, there are times when technical skills will not be the top of your priorities and are replaced by wider qualities, particularly potential. You may well rank colleagues' softer attributes such as facing change with equanimity above qualifications and possibly even track record. As chief executive you may need to take the risk to appoint from outside or promote someone within 'above' their colleagues, based on your requirements and the candidates' capacity for growth. Such decisions can be particularly difficult for the people you don't promote if they have absolutely provided what the organisation has needed in the past, and who might even have contributed to the organisation now being in a strong place, a place in which their skills, ironically, are now less central. Partly because of the bruise being inflicted to their sense of self and partly of course because of the financial and career insecurity which has just opened up, the individual may lack the capacity truly to perceive the changed organisational needs and to accept the need to create space for new talent. The person may feel that their dedication is as strong as ever, that they are the same, achieving employee and so, why are they being challenged? This can result in bewilderment and resentment. But you are demonstrating a critical crucial leadership quality: distinguishing what skills (and behaviours) are critical now, what can be learnt by others and who to move where. Recognising and placing someone for their potential, aptitude and attitudes are key chief executive functions, and recruitment, particularly from internal sources, mostly involves disappointing someone. Let me describe some scenarios which can forces active management of roles.

You've looked, with the board, at the strategic position of the organisation and come to a clearer view about what needs to happen to take forward its work over the next period. This might be tangible and straightforward things, such as shifting resources towards what is already successful, without too much adjustment in *how* this activity is done. Perhaps you just need to market more deeply to your core audience and the skills you have to do this are strong, just needing a bit of shifting around. Possibly extraneous but (internally) popular activity has to reduce.

More likely, however, you will have noticed something a little harder to shift, for example that the outside world is talking about your business in a different language from that used internally. Stakeholders and customers might be saying that they know your brand and respect it, but in a rather general way, rather than actually identifying with it or feeling attached to it. (All modern marketing is now very much focused on customers 'belonging' to the brand, rather than just consuming it). When you probe further you may find that internally moving with this trend is greeted with some impatience: 'We have a great product, we are respected, we have worked really hard to get that respect – we are doing the right things!' This may particularly be the case if you have a longstanding and indeed successful team which has built up the business to a certain place. What you need now is a bit of critical professionalism to review the ownership of the brand by customers and you particularly need this objectivity in the senior team. You need people who are not fazed by looking at the market and the competition and who are looking forwards, not backwards. This is a point to remind yourself that you, as chief executive, are the custodian of the long-term evolution of the business. Guaranteeing this secures the livelihoods of those within the business and the satisfaction of the customers for whom it exists. You have to have open and forward-looking people in key roles. This might argue for promoting newcomers who have less in-built affection for the company. They, ironically, are the ones who may be best-placed to work out how to build that affection in the outside world.

An engineer was talking to me recently about what he observed in science laboratories, particularly those with public backing. They are typically established by clever people, and have a clear remit and state-of-the-art facilities. For up to twenty years or so they can lead their field, but their very cohesiveness and the kinds of people that make them strong initially may, in the long term, make them myopic about the wider world. Facilities may become outdated and perhaps there is a cultural, psychological dimension here: many scientists, like most researchers, will like conditions of relative stability and regularity so that they can pursue their own deepening research agendas. After about twenty years it is likely that they are at risk of being unresponsive to pressing issues beyond the lab walls. In the world of publicly-supported laboratories, my contact observed, it seemed as if there was often a deliberate shake-up by funders of contracts and locations for key work. This is massively disruptive and demoralising for those who are on the wrong end of it, but perhaps the system needs a creative upheaval to renew itself.

What you, as chief executive, are charged with is to avoid the ossification of your organisation or company so that it is at this kind of risk from your market, whatever this is. As with the forester choosing a variety of species over monoculture and to some extent having to anticipate an unknown future, you need to build the capacity for adaptation and making bold choices, not just for continuing to deliver your business as you have done to date. To do that you have to ask what aptitudes, casts of mind and qualities need to be nurtured or brought in. This is about more than skills and knowledge. I am talking about such capabilities as:

- the ability to think strategically and laterally.

- the confidence to listen to what customers are saying without feeling threatened.

- the enjoyment of 'skilling-up' to meet new demands.

- the ability to scan good practice elsewhere fairly quickly and draw conclusions from it.

- a winsome way with colleagues and external contacts.

Only you will know quite what the comparable list is for your organisation. It may take an amount of skill and courage to move in this direction and how you do so will depend on the ground rules of your company or organisation.

Assuming that you are need to do some pruning, thinning or redesign, there are some things which will make the labour of a restructure of whatever scale easier:

- Trust your instinct on what behaviours and aptitudes you want to grow or prune, once you've had the conversations with colleagues, the board and stakeholders.

- Construct your own list of the three internal and three external things you want to be different as a result of any change. Be precise with these indicators, for example, more relaxed conversations between teams, calendars that have more networking and speculative meetings in them, sales, turnover.

- Don't sound too hippy however. Keep referring back in every key conversation to the big boulders which your organisation needs to move, so that these are familiar to your team when you refer to them later, as justifiable reasons for moving people around.

- Overcommunicate with your senior management team and have regular one-to-ones with those who appear to be most mystified or who are likely to be resistant.

- Once you know that a change is required keep saying why, specifically; the necessity and the gains to be had. What won't happen if the change is not made? What opportunities, precisely, come from the changes, for the business and for colleagues in their work?

- Ensure you have cover and support from your chair and board.

- Be bold and make decisions; but give time for people to react and opportunities to respond. Remember that no-one is where you are on this, because you are the leader and ahead of everyone else in understanding. You should be sensitive to this, whilst using your vantage point to reassure people about the future. This is a staggered, uneven bereavement. Anonymous questionnaires are useful.

- Follow best HR practice, and keep everything you do legal. You must not ease people out who should have had help to perform better, under the guise that their job is changing so much they could not possibly fit it. Restructuring and performance improvement are separate things, and you need to insist that they remain separate even when tempted to save money and particularly time by conflating them.

From experience, telling people that their posts are no longer needed is tough, very tough. But as Eleanor Roosevelt counselled, 'You gain strength, courage and confidence by every experience in which you really stop to look fear in the face. You must do the thing you think you cannot do'. (You Learn by Living, Eleven Keys for a More Fulfilling Life). There are ways of doing this conversation well and ways of doing it badly. Writing things carefully, keeping to timetables and giving people some slack around the harsh times are all important. And in most cases I have been involved in, new and possibly better avenues have opened up for colleagues, I am thankful to say. Those left may feel something akin to 'survivor guilt' but this is reduced if good outcomes emerge for those who left and also if chief executive communication is very much about a productive, outward-facing future; the 'why' of pain always makes it much more bearable. This is another take on the theme of depersonalisation as a key leadership tool: lifting the narrative to the higher ground of your organisation's purpose and future gives you space to manage, while the emotion swirls around. It does not mean you are indifferent to the human cost and indeed you should say, repeatedly, that change, whilst difficult, is the greatest guarantee of a good future, for current and future employees.

At the beginning of the last chapter I suggested a change journey from conversation, to the deployment of people, to changing structures and governance. Moving to the last two, without which a change process is not complete, the McKinsey 7s framework is a perennial tool for assessing organisational essentials *in relation to each other*, covering structure and governance, and if you haven't discovered it, now might be a good time to Google it. It proposes seven aspects of the well-functioning organisation, all conveniently beginning with 's', with 'shared values' in the centre, linking all of them. Strategy is just one of the aspects and should not dominate at the expense of shared values, style, systems, staff, skills and, last but not least, structure. When interrogated against each other, the seven aspects provide something like a balanced scorecard of an organisation's position, a useful spur for discussion by the executive team and the board (separately and/or together) to assess the balance of strengths in an organisation. Once again it is a tool to depersonalise issues and come to a shared, objective view, which legitimises difficult decisions.

Using the framework might show that, given staffing, strategy and the values of the organisation, the structure is top heavy, in the size of the board, or number of committees; or, alternatively, it might be felt too light to serve emerging activity. The symptoms and results of such an imbalance can be major decisions not sufficiently scrutinised or conversely too much time spent batting decisions round various committees and the executive. Here are some reflections on the role of the chief executive towards structure and governance and their implications.

Firstly, it is something that will take your time at certain points, even if the behind-the-scenes role of an effective chief executive sorting out the 'plumbing' rightly stays behind the scenes. The chief executive of a major national housing charity may be on the news passionately conveying the latter's position on the latest policy (or lack of it) on social housing. This is what many people think chief executives do, most of the time. In reality, it will take colleagues a few hours to get the messaging right, less time to brief the chief executive, still less time for her or him to do the media outing. By contrast, days and weeks might be taken restructuring governance, to include the balance of board and committees (and even which of the latter is still needed), who chairs them, who they report to, their 'delegations' (their power) – and so on. It is another example of where management and leadership are bedfellows; it takes a lot of leadership to reconfigure where the power is held, partly because it is where a lot of people (including board members) can and do get very wound up about their influence and how they are perceived by their peers. The chief executive will make sure there is the space to have the debate at the senior level and will advise the chair on the implications of options, business and individual. This advice is only sound if the management implications are understood, such as the amount of time the new arrangements will take to service, and it is not a simple management task to get the whole governance system right. Yet it is all worth it; without it the best strategy and leadership will lose pace, something akin to the loss of suction power in a vacuum cleaner as the bag fills with dust. To someone with little experience of how organisational governance works this quite understandably seems arcane and perhaps bureaucratic, the kind of thing a donor to a charity doesn't want to feel she is paying for. But good governance is crucial for the effectiveness of his or her donations and the mission, and the buck for good organisational structure should stop with the chief executive and chair. It can't be fully delegated elsewhere. It is right to spend some of the boss's salary in sorting these things out, with further senior salaries expended as needed.

It is useful to be aware of how varied governance models can be in different sectors and anticipate that at some point in your career you will need to navigate your way through options for your organisation. It is not the most exciting area for a typical chief executive, but it is a solid aspect of a good legacy for your successor, a foundation for any organisation's sustainable future. Good governance on leaving should be included in your aims for your time in post, even if the decision is that no change is needed.

An NHS hospital trust board will have both executive and (paid) non-executives on it, chaired by a paid non-executive. By contrast, the Charity Commission is keen that only in exceptional circumstances should a trustee of a charity be paid, which will tend to mean that a charity chief executive is not also a trustee and, however much time a chair puts in, he or she is not remunerated. However, where a charity is substantially publicly funded and is therefore akin to an arm's length body (at arm's length from government but fulfilling government objectives) or quango, the chief executive is appointed with the approval of government, and the chief executive might be required by government, as the main funder, to be on the board as a measure of control over public funds. There are also charities where the governing body is all paid, for example typically in Oxbridge colleges where, by statute, the Head of College and Fellows make up the Governing Body, with no external members.

In the private sector, a company's Chair is likely to be remunerated but the board will be much more selective than an Oxbridge college governing body. Involving all teaching staff in the governing body of a college is as if all medical staff of a hospital are on the board, which seems a recipe for disaster. However, an Oxbridge college will be smaller and based on the principle of an academic fellowship of equals. A committee structure is often used to brings matters to the governing body for final decision. A college culture may not be sympathetic to a high level of delegation (because the teaching staff is the collective leadership), and there may be no equivalent of a senior management team, rather these committees, dealing with, but not making final decisions about, particular areas. Therefore the chair of an Oxbridge Governing Body, likely to be the Head of College, may spend a lot of his or her time ensuring that committees are functioning well, so that the Governing Body can make sound decisions from their recommendations. This can be onerous, compared with a chief executive able to work with a senior executive team preparing papers for a non-executive board (more common in the charitable and parts of the public sector).

The best chief executive will exercise patience and deep breathing as he or she plugs away at reconfiguring the shape of the organisation, particularly since some colleagues might still be feeling the effects of a wider change process, of which this is the last stage. (I made the point earlier about being sensitive to the time lag between your experience and those around you; you are always ahead of others, and their experience of change may be much more traumatic than yours). I know of one Head of College who spent a lot of her time reducing the governance and who met with some resistance, particularly as the power to make those changes is not entirely clear; the Head of College is a focus for leadership but does not have power to direct. But it was appropriate for her to address the effective functioning of the college and she persisted. Another Head of College told me of the 'diplomatic capital' he felt he had to build up, and spend judiciously, to get this kind of business done. He also however, seemed to keep some kind of tally about the amount of time it was taking and a skilful chief executive will be decisive and require decisiveness from others when any new arrangements really do need to be sorted and their benefits begin to be felt.

The next chapter deals with values and culture, practical and positive aspects of the working life and another means to steer through times of change.

Chapter 6

Values and culture: practical business tools

'Organisational values and culture' tends to be the suitcase in which we pack all the things that haven't quite fitted into our management and leadership categories. We sort of know they are important, but discussion is often vague and disconnected from the nitty gritty of management decisions, still less daily practice. But what if this is what distinguishes one organisation from another, central to how we attract and retain employees, critical to building customer loyalty and crucial to how we guarantee resilience when the going gets tough? Because I believe this is what values and culture do, I would put them right there on the list of mainstream management tools, and as a chief executive would spend time and thought on how they translate in practical and business terms.

Values and culture are really the norms of an organisation or group, its default ways of operating, whether it's a Prime Ministerial Cabinet, a hospital or a corner garage. They are revealed in questions like:

- How does it feel to be here (for example relaxed or fraught, competitive or collaborative?)

- What kind of reward is really valued: monetary, relational, the working environment, pride in the services you provide, external standing and impact?

- When we say, during recruitment, 'This person will fit in well', what do we mean? What kind of person would really struggle here? Why?

- On what occasions would we not make apparently the best short-term business decision because it conflicts with deeper values?

- Which of the casual comments you overhear in the kitchen – about anything – do you as chief executive absolutely have to challenge?

Clearly there are no generalisable right or wrong answers to these questions. The answers will completely depend on the history and context of the organisation. But they are not set in stone and our role as leaders is to mould the values and cultures to work for the business in the short, medium and long-term. Attention to them protects against the kind of fraud and scandal which can bring down even the giants overnight. It reduces the waste caused by chasing targets rather than real outcomes of your mission. It grows the reputation of your organisation and therefore its supporters and customers. It encourages the best people to stay and makes the less able people uncomfortable.

So let me unpack the often-evaded values and culture discussion in order of difficulty.

I hope that in chapter 3, about the first year and performance management, you were persuaded that *how* people do their jobs should be embedded – with some precision – in the performance management framework. You might then want to develop a values statement for internal organisational practice, including something like: 'WE SHARE RESPONSIBILITY for a productive, purposeful and positive office atmosphere'. Sometimes the expression of the culture of a place does not extend beyond these daily behavioural norms and indeed if they are brought home in a practical way through discussion they can be very valuable, for example something like: 'We do not chat about soaps during the day – because we put serving our customers first'. However, whilst these day-to-day expectations *are* a potent signal of the wider cultural assumptions, they aren't enough by themselves to underpin acceptable and unacceptable behaviours.

Less straightforward to achieve but with more impact is setting out the basic moral position. This might be a little more challenging, if it has not been done before or is seen by colleagues as being irrelevant to the business. How central is integrity to your business and how is this expressed and protected? Who can actually decide this? It may be that it is not under your control and you can only influence, or leave. Thomas Cromwell, as readers of Hilary Mantel's novels have been compellingly reminded, was cumulatively manipulated by his boss into undoing people for whom he had respect and sympathy, compromising his integrity, until their fate also befell him. When Cromwell says to Henry that the case against Sir Thomas More is thin, Mantel has Henry say to Cromwell that he, Cromwell, is retained to be a viper; at that moment Cromwell knows knows how deeply he is in the mire. Of course the Tudor court is a particularly dark and dangerous example of organisational power play, and I would hope that you have rather more options if your chair compromised you to anything like that extent. However, the point holds, that understanding the lines in the sand beyond which you will not go, matters for your own integrity, and the future of the organisation.

Over the last decade, the financial sector has been the biggest single example of the potential for calamities that lies in not having an embedded moral position, followed through at all desks and found out if not. The public and not for profit sectors have also seen their fair share of a lack of probity, and some days we may wonder from where the emerging next generation will absorb its professional standards. The best we can do is to try not to put a foot wrong ourselves. I was once in a position where, after publication, I was told that a key figure for the organisation's achievement was inaccurate, and on the side of exaggeration. The figure did not look way out, but it would have been difficult to progress going forward and it was just wrong, and in the public domain. The error had come about due to a combination of marketeers outside the business being given more rein than they should have had, a lack of an internal 'enforcer' re-reading the text and my own relative inexperience, which meant that I did not know at what level I needed to check things out. I alerted my chair, as there was a potential reputational risk and a cost to sorting it out. We did find a way to rectify things, but not without some hassle and disgruntlement on the part of some colleagues (although it had been others who had alerted me to the issue). Looking back, this was a useful if bumpy moment which I was ultimately able to use to signal, early on, my zero tolerance of inaccurate information and the need for facts to trump hype.

There is plenty of evidence that not putting the truth first is, in the end, damaging to the business. Internally, if it is tolerated once or twice it will become accepted that the truth can be exaggerated or underperformance masked and sooner or later this will come back to bite everyone. (This corrosion happened at the sectoral level in the testing of diesel cars for particulate emissions). If you have to sacrifice short-term business objectives (ie lose money) to maintain integrity, then see it as an opportunity to put a marker in the sand for the longer term good. If you have to pull colleagues back at the last minute and irritate them in the process, see it as something you and they will learn from. Explain that exaggeration isn't good for trust between colleagues and with the outside world and this is a business issue. Look out for the deviations from the truth in apparently non-strategic things: straplines, images and their captions, tweets, websites, Christmas parties and expense claims, not just in the big documents and the mainstream tasks. Don't cede the scrutiny of these to others without having absolute confidence that they have the same level of non-tolerance as you. Perhaps the best analogy for how the culture of an organisation is gradually laid down is the English constitution, which proceeds by precedent and the accumulated norms which sink under our collective skin and are periodically tested. On an iterative, case-by-case basis, the chief executive, board and staff lay down, and live, an organisation's moral culture.

A postmodern perspective would of course assert that there is indeed more than one version of the truth and we must entertain multiple perspectives; the chief executive needs to be aware that one person's truth ('solid performance across the board' in an annual report) will be another person's evasion. Tolerance of 'imaginative' reporting will vary. I have a great loyalty and love for the unspectacular and generally self-deprecating and underestimated Midlands area of England. So when any company or organisation based there bursts forth in purple prose about spectacular achievement, stunning scenery or unique artistic verve, a bit of me really wants to go with it. (All hail the county council person who came up with 'Staffordshire, the creative county', which adorns all county boundary signs. THE creative county!) After all, other areas are likely to be making similarly rosy claims and some have the spectacular, such as the mighty sculpture, the Angel of the North, on their side. But there will be a line which you will not let colleagues cross: can the Midlands really claim to have the best inland waterways system in the world? Can the region not win people by it being remarkably accessible, full of its own heritage and charming in its own way? Exaggeration sometimes arises out of sloppiness, a wish to follow the crowd, a lack of real understanding of the product and its niche. Our product and its customers can cope with something better: thoughtfully presented reality.

To bring this point round to you personally as chief executive: never, ever, yourself write or speak a line which you can't say is true, or knowingly sign off on something from a colleague which you can't endorse. Ambiguity and vagueness are one thing – I hold my hand up to not always putting the truth down in detail at every point; it is part of the trade – but untruths are another. If you suspect something you are being asked to say is 'unevidenced', ask for the evidence.

More problematic still than the nuances of communication is where values and practice are in conflict, or at least not well-aligned – and whilst this is probably always the case to some degree, because values aspire to perfection and never achieve it, there comes a point where it is dangerous. For example a hospital will of course say that its values are patient-centred, demonstrated in the best clinical care, communication and patient choice. The day-to-day culture however is likely to be overshadowed by other demands for productivity and in reality it must feel as if another key, and yet conflicting, value, is dominant: 'The balanced budget is the ultimate good.'

What is often going on of course is that the culture is not supporting, or is actually in conflict with, the values. The values need to drive the culture, not vice versa. I know a project worker in an NGO, who had absolutely the same basic values about the cause as her colleagues, but who was exasperated on occasion by an intellectual culture inclined to discuss at depth and in detail. Deciding – in a very sophisticated way – whether or not to invite a donor to an event stopped the whole office in deep conversation for what felt like (and could be) hours on end. The discursive culture cut across the core value of operating efficiently for a client group with overwhelming needs. The working practice needed an injection of efficiency – in the name of the cause. As I write this, Jeremy Corbyn has become Labour leader and the tension between his aspiration for an open, democratic, free-for-all and the need for some level of discipline is evident: how far will he actually tolerate his shadow cabinet saying how much they disagree with him? The great dissonance between the two political virtues of discipline and freedom lies behind the fortunes of political parties over decades.

A poised chief executive will encourage colleagues to identify where values are not being supported in what goes on every day, or where values are in conflict, and then encourage that discussion without dominating it. Bringing this conflict out into the open might help get people using their 'values' muscles more routinely, although if I am being honest, I am not sure I have ever seen this throughout a team, probably because however much you want to be seen to be making a general point, values conversations may seem to implicate one particular person. Looking back I would want to have found a way round this, for example in team meetings, so that conversations are not just about what is going on but the why and the how. It's easier to talk about the details of a new office layout than whether we are really egalitarian enough to give everyone an open desk in a shared office.

Such deep work by a leader perhaps needs a happy conjunction of personal confidence and enough space to think and act, along with a supportive environment and senior team which is not fixated only on delivery. As chief executive you can help create the environment for the values work. As outlined earlier, no-one should be performance-managed only against quantitative targets: motivation for good behaviour, supporting the corporate ethic, should be in there too. Chief executive effectiveness in embedding values will also depend on your deepest motivation, your psychological strength and your personal maturity as leader. I wonder too if there are points in your career when it is easier to be assertive about values without being a dictator, accepting that they are the stuff of debate, conflict and raggedness? If you are going through a time in your life when your own values and beliefs are shifting (and chief executives are allowed these times as much as anyone else!) it may be harder to be assertive at work about behavioural norms, but this is still necessary. It is good to be aware of the interplay between moral leadership at work and the moral, personal journey outside it.

It is worth reflecting on how the chief executive's own principles can and should affect the values and culture of your workplace. From the outside, the job of the chief executive will tend to look more technical than it feels, with right and wrong approaches easy to recognise (at least in retrospect). There is certainly a set of things which a good chief executive needs to be able to do and a set of behaviours he or she needs to exhibit. But when you are in the role, it is riddled with your own conscious and less conscious principles and preoccupations, and you are colouring the role in the same way that an artist will choose his or her palette. A good chief executive – one with the personal maturity sufficient for the role – is likely to be one comfortable with his or her value systems. These provide ballast and direction, underpinning the role and protecting it from their whims and moods (their own, or those of others). A very good one is likely to be self-aware about these values and how they are to be brought into play, or not, in the organisation, and their impact, for good or bad. In my own case, openness and not playing games with people are important values. Occasionally I have to rein them in and be more tactical and circumspect, to enable due process to happen, or to make sure people came to conclusions themselves. Machiavelli, presumably, had the opposite issue.

William, previously a chief executive and now chair of a complex hospital trust, provides an interesting example of the challenges around bringing values to life in an organisation. At around the age of 50, he came to see that the conventional ways of talking about what a hospital should do, or perhaps needs to be, were clearly not enough to achieve what is required. The culture of measurement was thinning out other, important, stuff. Values of respecting each person and working as a team were there on paper but embodied only partially. Emboldened by suddenly realising he was no longer the young man on the up, but a seasoned leader whom people would listen to, he responded to the inner impulse to find a new language beyond the technocratic vocabulary for health service improvement. Social capital (notions of trust, exchange and common life) seemed to him to add something important to conventional key health performance indicators. He even risked talking about love as an alternative framework, a means and an end, both for services and for society more widely – and this was not coming from a specifically religious starting point. There will not be many chairs who could say: 'I am using the Non Executive Directors appraisal process to inch the other board members in the "love" direction'.

One might hesitate to try something similar earlier in one's career. There is something akin to 'track-record capital', which the more confident leader should trade in on occasion, taking a risk to say honestly that the old paradigms are not achieving the changes we want and proposing ideas which in a younger and less established person might be construed as touchy-feely. This is not to say that the concept fully landed for William. He looked, in new appointments, for the opportunity to find more traction for his ideas in sympathetic executives, thirsty for new ways of pushing practice.

To summarise this chapter, values, culture and behaviour are practical, day-to-day business issues. They are not just the work of inspirational leaders like Nelson Mandela or a pro-poor Pope who make a lot of people feel a bit more hopeful about the world. In any case, such figures are too remote from most of us to change behaviour: witness South Africa's struggles even when Mandela was still with us, and the continual leaching away of church membership. Just by being charismatic, caring or high-minded, you do not necessarily secure your organisation's legacy. The misdemeanours of every priest who has committed them have to be dealt with, to restore trust fully. I would assume (hope, perhaps) that Pope Francis has any number of difficult meetings reforming the Vatican, whilst appearing smiling on the balcony, and even so, the pace of change is not enough for many. Values work is done at the coalface. It is stimulated and enacted by leaders prepared to fret and muddy themselves in any number of very difficult conversations and restructures, taking a human and systems perspective of the change they want to enact.

Values and culture are anything but woolly or optional. In that vein, here are some places to get stuck in.

- The tone of voice in any notices on the walls: punitive, super-casual, full of emoticons or framed in black?

- The accuracy of any numbers going to the board, such as reporting against key performance indicators.

- The tone and content of anything said to the outside world, including annual report, website and social media.

- Spend in the most obscure, hitherto unscrutinised, budgets.

- Team meeting agendas: the balance between detailed updates on work, reflections on practice, areas to resolve, underlying principles.

- Recruitment: challenge any too easy assumption that 'fitting in' means 'being like us', but be clear what the core behaviours have to be.

Chapter 7

Closest colleagues: working with your senior team and line reports

On the London tube once, around 9.30pm, a Wednesday, I passed a work group, all youngish men, bar one who was older, saying good-bye to each other in ever so slightly dishevelled suits as they took their different lines home. They were a bit loud, a little oiled: office guys who'd had a drink or two after work. As a last goodbye, the oldest group member revealed himself to be the boss as he said, semi-joking, 'Don't be late in tomorrow!' The beneficiaries of the friendly command turned into their tunnel, which happened to be mine, and it is a good job that the boss couldn't hear the scornful (and admittedly slightly inebriated) guffaws: 'He couldn't stop himself, could he?' one asked. You can take the boss out of the office but, even at the end of a friendly night, you can't take the office out of the boss, it would seem. I have to admit that I completely recognised what the boss had been doing, more for himself than for them, perhaps; recovering the more comfortable territory, signalling that this social only came about through work, after all, reinstating his role ready for the morrow. Would there have been a difference if he'd said: 'See you in the morning – if I make it in!' and kept the laddish confidentiality of the night going a bit longer, with a bit of self-deprecation? Perhaps not and perhaps it does not matter. On balance I think the boss was more on the right than wrong side of the line; in the end, the work relationship trumps the friendliness which should go alongside it and some-times needs to be restated, preferably not clumsily – and this is easier to do sober. Maybe the best of all would have been to stay noticeably less inebriated than anyone else; actions could then speak louder than words, around expecting to be prompt in the following morning.

More generally, how should your organisation's boss relate to his or her line reports? Is it different from that of any senior manager with *their* line reports? At a senior level, after all, whether a manager or chief executive, you are always trying to deliver the wider business through your management relationships, having an eye for and com-municating corporate aims rather than just steering tasks, so there is no significant difference there. If anything, this delivery of corporate direction through line management should have just become a little easier compared with being second or third tier, as you are now especially well-sighted on the key business priorities you want to drive through your management relationships and it will be expected that you do so. Senior managers are often, if not flattered, at least made to feel part of a shared inner leadership ring when the chief executive is clearly deploying them to drive through critical business issues – and it is something to fret about if any of your reports are stuck at a lower, task-focussed, level than they should be operating at. Make sure reviews and job plans (chapter 3) are helping you here.

However the organisation's impact does not hinge just on your one-to-one relationships with your reports, but also on the senior management team you are likely to form with them. Such teams are, of course, most effective when they are close knit, underpinned by strong individual relationships between you and the others, but acting as a unit. In the most effective senior team, openness about the risks to the organisation, dealing with 'common enemies' (go with this idea, but watch it too, lest you encourage tribalism) and digging deep into the organisational quandaries, can create real strength and a cohesive approach. As you will know from the literature on emotional intelligence, the *quality* of self-knowledge, mutual sharing, empathy and disclosure fundamentally affects how effective working practices are, and this applies to the group as well as the individual. There is an element of mystery as well as technique in how this evolves, depending on who's there.

In a senior team, and in the divisions or departments its members head up, it's usual to find people behaving as if they are there to represent their specialism, be it fundraising or finance. I have great admiration for those breed of finance directors who not only hold the purse strings but can actually *propose* spend, seeing where there is underinvestment against the strategy. Similarly, as per the previous chapter, I admire marketing colleagues who can embrace ambiguity and truly care about reflecting the nuances of a policy position, not just pump out the messages which will attract the most social media likes. These people do exist! But you will recognise the point I am making: managing a senior team is often about stopping it from becoming a succession of caricatured positions. You are busy keeping the channels between them open and trying to get them to come together in a fresh way around the main challenges.

Bringing the differences in the senior management team out into the open can of course be useful and it is the chief executive (or an external facilitator) who can be seen to be doing this with no vested interest. One environmental business I know has both a London and a provincial (a word which for me as a Midland girl is something of a badge of honour) office. The purists for the cause are in London. They are the ideologists, no doubt with a fair few masters degrees between them. They would be the ones to say no to any sponsorship that might sully the brand, confident that they can get other investment in, being in the capital. The provincial team is very embedded locally, has a lot lower turnover, and is there to practice the art of the possible. They are suspicious of highmindedness, preferring to be the high priests and priestesses of pragmatism. With whatever background and cultural differences you have, perhaps the best bet is to name them, articulate their strengths, get it out on the table that people are coming from different contexts and see how much difference in approach is allowable and even beneficial.

There is plenty of good stuff in the management literature about leading a team and I hope you will enjoy periodic web and book searches into that rich vein. Instead, here I turn to how and when you dip into the work of others at lower levels in the organisation as chief executive, possibly skipping a level or two beneath you. In my experience, it is an area in which to show confidence and find courage, even though you have to negotiate the levels in between in doing so. 'Walking the floor' is, rightly, standard advice in the management library and this can be done in physical and other ways.

How much and when you intervene in operational activity will depend on so many things, including your expertise, the quality and training below you, whether there are changing external requirements best communicated by you, and so on. Frances, whom we met earlier benefiting from the reading matter of her Head of HR and deploying a trusted operations director within a multi-million pound national charity, is prepared to be seen to engage in operational issues, if only to show that she still (apologies, Frances!) knows how to do it. It should be a useful surprise to a new recruit under 40 that the boss can improve a briefing or sharpen a risk analysis around a technical issue; it will keep them on their mettle to see that your seniority is founded on a grasp of the operational.

To reiterate a recurring theme of the book that what is important is what is important, not what is labelled 'strategic', it is not your job to float above operations under the mantra 'bosses are strategic and never meddle', but nor should you take away or try to do the jobs of other people, even if you can do them. As with the discussion of the board, you should simply be concerned with what is significant for now and the future, and who does that, rather than with fine distinctions between the strategic and the operational. In the field of forestry, a quintessential example for leaders is the control of things which harm woodland. These tend to be deer, grey squirrels and disease. You may decide to do nothing and take the risk of destruction, or you may not. Either way, a responsible leader cannot sit back with no strategy, inadequate means to implement a strategy or, in the worst cases, no story about why the threat can't really be avoided (which is the case with the relative newcomer to Britain, ash dieback, which is wind-borne). The asset may go to ruin, or, if you do well in protecting the asset by controlling grey squirrels, you may be charged with cruelty (albeit by a public mostly consuming intensively reared animals who have a much worse time). The buck and the media response stop with you.

Much of this will be familiar to you if you have already had a senior management role, with tiers of activity beneath you. As chief executive, the added dimension is your unique vantage point, letting you 'go in' on those things that really matter for your organisation and directing resources with impartiality. My point is that chief executive interventions *could* include such micro level things as the use of certain individual words in a press release, one particular budget line and the order of an agenda to allow the important matters to have enough time. If your 'red pen' marks defend what is important, you have acted strategically and it is not unhelpful micro-management. Of course you should still coach about how colleagues handle important issues, at every opportunity, so that you are not taking these decisions because of a skills or confidence deficit.

It requires some discipline and energy to engage at this level, however, when there are any number of other priorities at the apparently more senior level. How tempting to assume that the people who need to know a good pitch to a client or, in the Civil Service, what the answer to a parliamentary question should look like, actually do. You might have total confidence that coaching in these tasks is going on systematically and what is being taught is what you would impart. But if you have seen even one inadequate example, you cannot have this total confidence. Looking back at my first year or so in one new post, I would have spent more time trying to identify which areas had the most embarrassment potential or risk if they were not being done well and interrogated these, wherever they sat in the organisation. I should have had more confidence with colleagues to say this was within my role as lead executive custodian of our strategy, mission and values. When you do get involved, it should always be possible to clearly say why you are focusing on certain areas – for organisational and not personal reasons.

A further tricky area, as evidenced by the boss on the tube, is the fine line between being friendly and being a friend; in the end, for me, whilst bringing your humanity into being the boss and encouraging relationships of trust, respect and openness – I hope one of the resonant themes of this book – you do just have to be able to manage. While in role as chief executive, you should model being a friendly professional, not a friend found at work. The universal tension in effective professional relationships, between closeness and the corporate – and the latter, in business terms, trumps human connectedness when the chips are down – is intensified at the chief executive level. Ultimately you need the space to make redundant, to reprimand and to sack, which you might be having to do 'at scale'. In particular you need objectivity and to be seen to be objective by your colleagues, whereas a team leader at a slightly lower level can possibly shelter under the boss's decisions when these difficult choices are made and preserve friendships more easily. I discussed this with someone recently promoted to a middle manager and he said that for him this was a new issue to consider. Not quite echoing the Wednesday evening on the tube which started this chapter, he'd been out on a night with his colleagues including line reports. He had not, up to this point, bothered about how coherent he had to be at the close of play. He had been surprised at how uncompromising a 'right-on' leadership trainer had been about this; never become the lad, maintain the space. I, boringly, tended to agree.

The price you pay for maintaining this line is periodic isolation, of course. PAs deserve a special mention here for reducing this isolation. Their inside take on what's preoccupying you, or at least the sense that you are preoccupied, gives a further reason compared with other colleagues to feel close to you and you to them. They have a particular empathy for your times of loneliness and the days when you are not so far from the end of the plank. If you are a PA, thank you. I cannot possibly see how some ratios between the lowest and highest paid employees in a company are justified. There is no rhetoric whatsoever in saying that there is absolute interdependence going on here.

Generalisations about what is acceptably friendly and what is un-acceptably pally don't work, given how different people and cultures are. It is through small and large acts that people come to understand your boundaries as boss, human being and friendly not-quite friend. My boundaries between friendly professionalism and being a friend would be signalled by the following, for your reflection, adaptation or rejection:

- You quite often start a one-to-one catch up with a colleague by asking after home or personal things, if they seem to want to share this, and you might refer to them briefly in closing, but in between you turn on the work switch and steel yourself to address today's issues, unless your colleague really is in a tough place. Where she or he is in a very difficult place, try to identify sources of support, rather than being drawn into giving it directly yourself.

- You don't see any member of the team regularly socially outside work, one-to-one. You are discreet about any social times with a small group of colleagues which are not part of official team socials. In my case, an occasional small group outing to see dance really wouldn't have floated the boat of many other colleagues and it was not a closed group, but still, it was a link shared just with a few and not something we chatted about at work.

- You do join in – and sometimes suggest – shared office social events.

- You are self-aware around any natural affinity with some colleagues and are scrupulous in not favouritising them, or being seen to do so.

- You ensure that policy on compassionate and family leave is fair and implemented fairly.

- In the softer, more social aspects of the role, you continue to be aware of the self you are revealing, following on from what you have done from arrival (Chapter 3). The friendliness signals you give – any gifts, messages or things that you do with others, need to add comfortably to the picture you are painting of yourself. You are thoughtful about what you share of your own experiences.

- If others' work friendships shade into something more intense, with colleagues apparently getting romantically embroiled, especially if they are not both single, and this being noticed by others, use a business rationale ('None of us should distract colleagues') to help stop it being unhelpful in the office. Do not become a counsellor. The distraction and discomfort caused to others can be significant and is sufficient justification for a word. Your actions are separate from any thoughts you may have as an individual on their situation. Less intensely, you may have relatives working in the organisation. Any line management responsibilities are best avoided, it seems to me, but then I have never worked in a family-owned business. It must be possible.

- If you are involved in an affair of the heart at work whilst chief executive or a senior manager, let's hope it's far from self-destructive: who knows, it may be the best thing of your life. But assuming it's reciprocated and it seems to be going somewhere, my expectation is that one of you leaves, fairly promptly. It's just too much for others to handle, unless you really are separated by Chinese walls, in a big organisation, are not seen together, and have no work overlaps, but this last point is I think impossible to achieve fully, however much formal distance there is. A chief executive has to be in a position to endorse and uphold difficult personnel and performance issues across an organisation. What if a restructure indicated that your partner's job had to go, or her boss's, which would give your partner a promotion opportunity. Would that departure seem objective? Even with the best Chinese walls, I have heard of such relationships held to be fine at the time, but, after one or both parties have left, people saying how odd and difficult it was. In the end your objectivity is compromised and my view is that it is not tenable.

Finally, though the message of the chapter has been professional poise whilst working with your colleagues, be open to how readily the management relationship fades and new opportunities to connect with some of your former colleagues open up. You may be surprised at the straightforward pleasures of an occasional text about family or other delights of normal life, after all those hard-won conversations, meetings and emails...

Chapter 8

You still have bosses: Chair and board

I was recently on the phone with a friend, a chief executive who had built up a not-for-profit and done enormously well, generating new income and raising the profile, over many years, through thick and thin. In his late 50s he was really struggling with his board, which he was finding critical of him and undermining. The trustees (the clue should be in the name) did not seem interested in witnessing the valuable activity going on and, in some cases, were more active in supporting their own businesses and other organisations. The chair was more absent than present and unable to contribute anything tangible. Most of my friend's executive team was probably blissfully unaware of the issues, but he was noticeably wrung out with it, dreading board meetings and, perhaps surprisingly for someone so apparently successful, conspicuously feeling the absence of the trustees' affirmation and tangible support. He wished the organisation was not entrusted to them.

I relate this in part to make the obvious point that in order to keep going successfully everyone, at whatever level, even chief executive, needs to feel valued at work. If, at the moment, your boss is the chief executive, an occasional compliment or word of encouragement in their direction, done subtly, is not a bad idea. A good chief executive doesn't need this every day however – a good thing, since it's improper to fan the flames of flattery in those around you on a daily basis. It is vital for an effective boss to cultivate her or his own techniques for valuing themselves, what we might call 'cognitive self-belief therapy', reminding themselves regularly of all they have achieved and from doing so drawing daily motivation and courage. But at times when a lot is hitting them, particularly things which are not in their power to resolve quickly, they will likely be depleting this battery store of self-belief. If you ever see a chief executive looking a bit tight between the eyes, it could be because she's caught on some draughty mezzanine between the needs of the team (very present) and those of the board (could be too present, could be too far away) with no-one supportively alongside: sometimes they just can't be. This is when the boss earns the salary and discovers whether they have any real, practical techniques for buoying up their sense of self.

These techniques are particularly needed in volatile and political environments, where the ultimate 'boss' is likely to be ducking and diving and trying to survive. A leader (ie the political head of a vast local authority) once said to me: 'Well Sophie they keep saying "the centre" and they mean me, but *I* don't know where the power is'. Senior officers are there to advise and caution their political masters and mistresses and deliver what is presented to the electorate as a long-term game plan, but in reality any Monday morning (or Sunday afternoon) can herald any kind of change as 'the centre' wobbles and gets diverted. This makes the chief executive or middle management role in a political environment particularly demanding; handling unpredictable demands from above and yet, as in all leadership roles, needing to be predictably supportive to your reports. It is not surprising that very able people in political environments become somewhat timid and risk-averse in office hours and prone, outside them, to taking up relaxing hobbies with particular dedication. I was much taken with how fervently a senior Whitehall bureaucrat (which is not in my book a disparaging word) defended her suburban choir night. As a chief executive you will need your equivalent, reliably restorative, activities.

Therefore, if as chief executive, you have as your bosses a chair and board which act as 'critical friends', rather than politicians who primarily need you for their political survival, you are fortunate and they are worth taking care of. I say more about this below. However before considering the mechanics, the example of my isolated and frustrated friend which opened this chapter also illustrates a less comfortable truth: that how a chief executive is getting on with his or her board is not independent from how well the job is fitting the person at this point. On the bell curve of an appointment, with effectiveness in the vertical axis and time on the horizontal, once the curve is going down (and the reasons for this are covered in Chapter 11), a chief executive's energy to invest in good relationships with what by then might be their third set of people round the board table is likely to diminish. He or she may wonder if they really have to explain once again the founding principles of the business, or why the organisation doesn't do more national advertising, or why the landlord won't change the office carpet for free.

When you are new to a job and at an earlier point in your career, there is inherent interest in the board relationship; it's a new skill area, after all, and there is some adrenalin around being the key person relating to the board, one of the main signs of your promotion. You are probably more open to taking a steer and learning from your bosses than later on, when it can be a different story. You might know that it will be a big education job to get the level of board support you want, given that you are more confident and experienced and do not need the level of input that is more immediately on offer. You may feel with some justification that your analyses are too sophisticated for them. But it does not mean that all their perspectives are wrong and that you can afford to ignore them; some simple messages about direction might need to be communicated, and heard, again and again. I write just after the Chilcot Report was published in the UK, with its analysis of how the country went to war with Iraq. It is said that Prime Ministers into their second or even third term, and after their departures, will increasingly declare that they harken to God or history (or their versions of the same), which together endorse their legacy in the face of other evidence. They are less keen on hearing from their colleagues. Herein lies danger for all of us. Perhaps it would be fair to say that board members need to work harder with the experienced chief executive, upping the quality of their listening and their questions, whilst the chief executive needs to dig into his or her reserves of patience and humility.

Returning to the beginning of the relationship between chief executive and chair, in the same way that a chief executive benefits from assertive line reports who express their needs and sometimes manage upwards, the chair will benefit from the chief executive taking the initiative about how you will work together. To be frank, the perils of a portfolio career, typical of a chair (and I speak as one) are manifold: a tendency to obsess about travel arrangements and how to fit in all these super-important non-executive meetings around holidays and other commitments; difficulty in distinguishing one set of issues in one organisation with similar ones in another in which one is also involved; not finding quite enough time to read the papers in advance of a pre-board phone call, but feeling you should do the phone call anyway; a belief that this flexible role can be fulfilled without structure; embarrassment about saying you've forgotten a fact or figure. It goes on. Meanwhile, the beleaguered chief executive 'just' wants the chair to get back promptly on issues, remember the key issues exercising the organisation (but ask for reminders without feeling it's a failure), keep to arrangements wherever possible and give a steer when needed, not just when irritated. Being assertive about your needs as a chief executive, early on, is entirely legitimate and core to the effective well-functioning of the organisation, so long as you expect the chair to do the same.

It should be simple, but it isn't always and any two chairs of the same organisation will play the relationship very differently, which makes me rather sceptical about books and courses which generalise about the relationship. I remember with one chair thinking that she'd like me to confide some personal news as an, albeit fairly crude, bonding mechanism and a reassurance that there was more to me than work. 'Would you like some gossip?' I asked. 'Oh yes please! I certainly do gossip', she replied (eyes shining). When I imparted the admittedly paltry personal titbit her face fell and I realised that she had no interest in that side of my life, whereas if it had been political 'gossip' – who was out and who was in – she would very much have enjoyed it. Other chairs however will find it hard to get into the substance without sharing some kind of life data. A mature and skilful chief executive will steer the relationship back to the core one of accountability, having imparted enough life data to satisfy human interaction and curiosity, maintaining a bond but reducing the time spent on this if it is in danger of dominating.

Moving to practicalities, it is vital to agree the modus operandi between chair and chief executive early on and of course every time there is a new chair, in a meeting where this is the central item. Here are some key areas.

One is around the nuts and bolts of the working relationship, such as frequency of contact, time of day for catch ups (compromises needed here), who rings whom, whether an agenda is sent in advance and so on. There are no rules around this, obviously, it depending on whether the organisation is in steady state, but you both have needs and a right to say what works for you. In my experience some regular arrangement is usually put in place eventually, so you may as well try to instigate it early, with the necessary degree of flexibility. If you have a chair who cannot commit to this I would not give in too quickly, but if it really proves impossible, the best you can do is dig around for times when you know you are more likely to catch her or him. You can always ask when is definitely not a good time and when, conversely, they are more likely to be on email or to pick up the phone. As chair I always say that if I answer the phone it is convenient and if not I will not answer but I will pick up the message, so never hesitate to ring if needed. I hope your chair would say something similar.

Another area is protocols for external contacts, for example who signs letters to whom (regardless of whether you have drafted them). I was once pulled up for communicating at Ministerial level when it should have been the chair, which was quite right in that particular world, even though another chair might have been glad to cede the 'privilege'. It would have been better to have established that earlier on, rather than have to learn through error.

A third issue is also external-facing: who 'fronts' the organisation at events. It would be more conventional in my world for the chair to MC a significant event and give top level messages, and the chief executive to present substantive information. Of course, this may shift from event to event, also, but it is useful to have an initial conversation about it, early on. You don't have to be too precious about it and even if the chair does present, most people in the audience at an event will know who to credit for the event and the wider work going on. There have been events where I have done the main address as chief executive and others where that has been the role of the chair. But if it is a big set piece event fronted by the chair, even if he or she says 'just notes please', you have to find a way of making sure the content and the tone are right. Sometimes drafting the full speech or presentation for the chair is acceptable and pays dividends. I allowed myself a moment of silent pleasure after one event where the chair had faithfully, convincingly and enthusiastically delivered verbatim a speech I'd drafted, as opposed to the bullet points I usually prepared, and a punter said: 'He really came into his own, today, didn't he?'

Everyone happy, then; the business got the right messages out there, the chair came over powerfully and the audience felt in the hands of someone with ownership of the mission.

Board meetings are of course the key building blocks of the organisational year. One of your jobs is to help the chair lead the meetings so the outcomes of the discussions can actually be received by and acted upon by the executive team. A board prone to be discursive will be helped by an agenda that clearly states where a decision is to be made. If the chair is not the world's most natural summariser of discussion, then establish in your early discussions whether he or she is happy for you to check (more accurately, propose, in some instances) 'what will be minuted' at the end of substantive items. This is code for relaying and summarising the discussion, a powerful moment which needs to be handled with respect. You can be seen to give eye contact and a 'check in' with the chair as you do it. Some chairs will welcome your lead, others may be a little affronted, but that might help them up their game in this respect. The first job of a chair is… to chair the meetings and this requires shaping and summarising each agenda item.

More widely, a chief executive, in my experience, longs for a board to ask questions which show an appetite for understanding the core business and the essential issues surrounding key decisions. Fair enough if, after these kinds of questions, board members go in hard to probe the options, but once more the focus on the truly important – not the easy, lower level niggly matters – should be what unites executive and non-executive at the board table. To liberate as much time as possible for this key discussion, you also need to agree what level and kind of questions should be asked in advance. If questions of clarification are dealt with outside the meeting, the more tactical and strategic probing can enjoy more time in the actual board meeting. You also need to ask yourself when reading final versions of the papers for the meeting how much temptation for the trivial you are putting in front of the board. You have a lot of responsibility for the level of discussion which takes place.

A chief executive is fortunate if the chair understands not only that the role is one step away from the everyday detail, but also that his or her role is necessarily not part of the executive team. The chair's team is the board, not the senior management team. William, chairing a hospital trust as well as running his own business, maintained this distinction to the extent of not going to the retirement party of his chief executive, which one hopes was interpreted as a sign of respect more than a snub. The degree of separation between chair and the executive is a cultural matter, an indicator of how much demarcation goes on versus pallyness, A new chair can make a blunder outside board meetings more easily than within them, and in this instance I would have thought the retiring chief executive, directly or through colleagues, could signal if the presence of the chair would actually be welcome, for at least part of such a gathering, to reflect the significance and the appreciation of the board, to wider colleagues as much as anything.

The basic point is that the chair is not 'part of the gang' and with a chair who is operating at the other end of the axis from William, that is to say a too-pally chair, the chief executive will need to find ways to reiterate that point, sometimes needing to cajole the chair to fulfil the formal, line management role which, although irritating on occasion (as these relationships are meant to be), is an essential for the chief executive. Sadly one hears of too many chairs who are inexperienced in or bored by this essential chair function (coming second after the ability to chair meetings), and who therefore interfere with the work of their chief executive, rather than support it.

In the rest of this chapter I will cover some of the practicalities and procedures to address early on, so that board meetings run smoothly.

- A quick survey of board members' views and current needs might be a good signal of your wish to get such things as the frequency of meetings, venue and the management of business spot on. It gives them an opportunity to voice the changes they wish to see with your arrival. As you receive replies, you can ponder what they tell you about the confidence of the board in its operation and its appetite for change. Make sure you leave an open, 'Any other suggestions', section. Check how well the board as a whole feels linked to its committees and how well their reporting is working for the board as a whole.

- Agree basics arrangements with the chair, such as how far in advance papers go out, whether clarifications to papers from board members are welcomed before the meeting and whether any other business items are to be notified in advance. This may involve revising board terms of reference and modus operandi. Check happiness with the format in which papers are being sent, eg hard copy vs electronic, and their formatting. I, for example, as a chair, dislike only having electronic copy as it's not great to chair via a laptop with a lot of papers, but other members of a board may be happy with an electronic set.

- Check that there is a list of the annual cycle or timetable for recurring and anticipated board papers, to include the signing off of the annual report and accounts, and confirm with senior colleagues and chair that the list still looks sensible, given any issues known to be coming up. Make sure colleagues responsible for any of the programmed papers are aware of what they need to produce when and, if you are able to, have a look in advance at last year's versions to see if you will want any changes. Colleagues will feel they are doing well to timetable in this probably rather tedious job and the last thing they want is to be told late in the day that the structure or length needs to be changed. (Some people are trigger-happy, others are more template-happy).

- If there is no meeting once a year with a less business-focused agenda (I would usually know this as an awayday), discuss with the chair whether this would be useful and feasible. Certainly these can be useful for horizon-scanning and getting the board to gel more closely together.

- Check that there is an up-to-date list of when members were recruited to the board and to committees, so that you know what succession planning is needed. Keeping a reasonable list of the skills and experience of the board is important – and if you do not have fixed terms of office, remedy that as a matter of urgency. A stale board will be a threat to your organisation, and is not best practice. Where you have ex-officio or representative members from other bodies, be watchful about a substitute always being sent; you may need to strengthen links or alternatively review whether the post is really appropriate.

- Work out an effective quality assurance process for the papers. It is not enough for one person to collate the papers and get them out (by post or electronically) without another person checking them. It is not enough for you to trust that all will be well in the hands of one person. Danger areas range from papers missing to bizarre page numbering, inconsistencies between papers (especially around the numbers) and gaffs at all levels, from a wrong spelling to a poor policy proposal, which will set cats among pigeons. Typically the three people for checking are yourself, the lead governance officer and a senior administrative person. It is for you to decide who does what, not the lead governance officer. Leave enough time to raise points with the authors of papers, especially cross-checking between them.

- Before your first board meeting instigate any improvements you can see to the presentation of agenda and papers, such as including the purpose of agenda items ('to agree', 'for information' etc) and effective cover notes. I adopted 'Purpose, Background and Recommendation (sometimes 'response')' or PBR, as the basic format for cover notes some years ago, having met it on a board I served on. Each of these sections should be brief; the acid test is whether the note enables a new board member to navigate the accompanying paper. Minutes can also be sharpened by the inclusion of actions, with initials, if this is not already being done. This makes dealing with 'matters arising' much easier. Don't leave it too close to the next meeting to check whether actions have been done! Delegate the request for updates on actions where appropriate, leaving plenty of time and make sure you get to see the results.

- Consciously vary the forms of the papers where you can, for example very brief notes just asking for immediate responses, to give a general steer, to more analytic options appraisals, with weighted scoring for issues to be considered. But keep the overall presentation consistent.

- The 'PBR' note also supports coaching your colleagues in writing papers. The latter should never be an account of everything that is going on in a certain area, nor an opportunity to prove how busy a person has been, tempting though this seems to be, from my experience of editing papers. Occasionally a narrative is needed, but this is likely to go into an appendix and the body of the paper is then free to focus on the question to the board, which demands a response. Asking colleagues to submit PBR notes in advance of the whole paper is an easy way to agree the why and how of the paper and to see who needs extra support in crafting a coherent paper.

- The role of the chief executive and indeed any senior team members present at board meetings needs clarity and is a good subject for your board survey and/or discussion with the chair. Are they advisors, full members, facilitators? How much does the chair welcome their unprompted input? It is best to have this out in the open and to expect that there could be shifts in what has gone before, with the board wanting to flex its muscles more, or, equally, wanting more input and guidance. I have worked with very different preferences from chairs in similar organisations and boards with apparently quite similar make up.

- If there is agreement that senior staff members do attend and contribute to board meetings, encourage structure in any verbal updates or presentation. The 'purpose, background, recommendation/response' principle applies in verbal contributions as well as in written papers, so coach colleagues to start with what you want to achieve through the input, give a reminder on where the matter has got to, including how the board has previously engaged with it, and finally ask for response or outcomes from board discussion. Threaten with severe penalty and double coffee duty anyone who introduces their paper with: 'Well, I think the paper is pretty self-explanatory, so I won't go into detail', and who then talks laboriously through it. You could perhaps distribute an image of a foot with a bullet hole in it as a sign of what has just happened, and a highlighter pen as a hint at what might change.

- At your first board meeting, be confident; you were appointed because the panel could imagine you at the board meeting, fulfilling this role, even if you feel inexperienced. Give the board its head where you can but if you need to shape something and pull them back from an ill-advised decision, do not hesitate just because it is your first meeting. You will only regret it later. The time-honoured 'Perhaps I could just add to that, in terms of [timescales/deliverability/the wider political context] …?' or similar is your trusty ally when you really need to head something off at the pass.

- Feed back anything difficult from each board meeting, from your perspective, to the chair promptly afterwards, for example the board going back in a cavalier fashion on an earlier decision which you have begun to enact, or a failure to listen to advice. Equally, ask your chair for and receive feedback on the papers and the meeting. Your work with the chair, especially pre and post board meetings, is an iterative process.

Finally, find the energy to empathise with your chair whatever the level of ease between you: he or she leads a team, in the same way that you have to lead yours. Perhaps your roles are not so different after all.

Chapter 9

Looking outwards: the external role

No-one is likely to have been appointed to a chief executive role if she or he cannot walk into a room or stand on a platform and make strangers believe in their organisation. When the chief executive walks out of that room or off the platform more people should feel that this is an organisation they would like to work with – or need to watch out for, because it's a strong competitor. Along with such set piece occasions, the external role is also of course about all the softer networking: the dinners, the awards, the conferences, travelling to see people on their own turf, being seen to care about your suppliers and partners' businesses. Such outward-facing advocacy, the representational function, should be seen as central and for many leaders it is indeed pretty instinctive, although there are good chief executives who have had to work hard at it. It is also a function that can be done in many different ways, depending on the personality of the chief executive, and it does not have to involve a whole lot of noise and back slapping. Any competent leader can know the selling points of their organisation, and be able to persuade others of them. But I think there are some holes into which I've fallen – and sometimes only just scrambled out of.

One simple hazard lies around the allocation of your time. An effective chief executive is responsive to his or her internal team and invests in them, with time and energy. I'm not implying self-sacrifice, like the pelican who is said to peck at its own breast to feed its young with its blood. But stating the obvious, and, as illustrated in this book, paying attention and giving time to key people in the business is how you get things done. The risk, though, and one which I have indulged, is that you run out of time (or feel you have run out of time) to look outwards and are responsive rather than proactive with external engagements, saying yes when you can go, but failing to plan external relations as proactively as you plan time with your colleagues. If you do not do this, you are likely to underperform on two of the three chief executives functions I listed early on: representation and protecting for the future. Perhaps seeing it like this is a helpful way to put some structure around how you invest in partner and stakeholder relationships. The following are examples of the kinds of external relationships that a chief executive in control of his or her diary would protect time for:

- Maintenance of the existing relationships which are part of the organisational furniture, even if not that exciting: for example, regularly touching base with Peter who is just about maintaining sanity as a middle-ranking 'minder' in your beleaguered main funding organisation and who is the gatekeeper for your future money.

- Investment in key relationships for the future: such as having a face to face with Edwin who has developed demand in a market you are moving into and can add intelligence and expertise to your organisation.

- Speculative contact with people who might ultimately matter to the organisation; perhaps a Skype with Miranda in Chicago whose brainy start-up may fail, but has some useful overlaps with your activities.

- Hanging out with people who inspire, encourage, challenge and warm you; make time for a drink with Aftab who always sees the good in your latest scheme, even if no-one else does.

- Being seen at the key conferences for your sector. At least go to part of them and make sure your organisation is clearly on the attendance list.

Once you have mapped your external priorities and as a result are finding yourself at a meeting or event which is, as far as you can be sure, worth your while, it does not necessarily take a lot of energy for a chief executive to be highly effective. It's an unavoidable unfairness to everyone else that a recognised leader has an easier path into a meeting of strangers than does a less senior person. Remember that people are glad just to have the chance to see the chief executive and make their point to you. It is demonstrating that you are similarly glad to meet them (and a happy chief executive *is* one who is genuinely interested in a wide range of causes and personalities) and being prepared to listen to their preoccupations which will score you the most points; usually there is no need to labour to rehearse your organisation's position. As a manager or senior manager you will often have been involved in a meeting for negotiations or attended meetings to agree programme or project work. Such meetings require talking, assuming an element of control and attention to detail. You may often still do these as chief executive, but one of the subtle shifts between the senior management and the chief executive role rests in how much, with the latter, 'just' giving time, absorbing views and offering warm but sometimes ever-so-slightly non-committal responses can rebound to the benefit of your organisation. In such external interactions, the significance of nodding, eye contact, saying 'uhuh' and asking after your contacts' latest issues cannot be understated.

It is generally prudent not to commit to anything substantive in a brief conversation at a conference and you can always, genuinely, ask for an email to follow up a particular issue, so you can discuss it properly with colleagues. A truly skilful chief executive will turn in a timely fashion from (genuine) listening and making the right level of commitments, to shaping and concluding a conversation and then moving on, all with their interlocutor not feeling short-changed in any way. Having said all this, as you travel to a venue, it is worth re-hearsing: what snippets of success or activity you will you want to use to indicate where you and your organisation are heading? Are there any live issues which will need handling if and when they come up? It isn't all about demonstrating that you are a good listener with no spinach between your teeth. (It's worth checking that one too, mind you, as the gums recede…)

One way to be particularly effective externally, possibly near the beginning of your time as chief executive, is to identify a strategic project led by one of your key partners or networks to which you can contribute. This has to have the support of your board, of course, which will be keen for the 'day job' to have your main attention. Early on in my career I worked for a new partnership of bodies trying to engage more deeply in a particular geographic area. I proposed working with an external organisation to help meet their agenda and to align our own project with its anti-poverty stand. But it became evident that my board did not want us to be 'helping' another organisation at this stage in the life of our project. They thought it would dilute our brand and an anti-poverty stand early on might not have commanded respect of their wider communities, who were gingerly waiting for my slightly left-field post to prove itself. The board did not in the end allow my time for it. The episode showed me the boundaries of our mission in the eyes of the board and the criteria for its support for external collaboration. More generally I learnt that this is something to check out properly in those kinds of ostensibly partnership roles.

More successfully, later in my career, we aligned important sustainability indicators at The National Forest – tracking things like river quality, GDP and employment – with government sustainability monitoring, demonstrating how national tracking of the social, environmental and economic well-being of the country could be adapted locally, making the monitoring much more useful. This collaboration earned us a bit of a reputation for technical competence and political nous within our government department, and the collaboration worked well both ways. In the private sector, this kind of opportunity may be more limited, but there are professional and other networks and initiatives across all sectors, which need strong contributions from member organisations. Finding the meta issues which make you and your sector look responsible and forward-looking is always worthwhile.

To conclude this chapter, there are four other points I would make, about the chief executive's advocacy and external role, from my own experience and shortcomings and with an emphasis on communication.

Firstly, feedback to the whole team on the messages from external events and networks is immeasurably valuable, even if most of your colleagues are not directly working with the same people. It is easy to forget how little time some of your team spend in the wider environment (in some cases, none, ironically often the people who answer the phones to the 'outside world' the most). Those who do have plenty of external contact will not be meeting all the same people as you. Even if the 'story' you bring back is quite trivial, such as an entertaining 'off message' moment between politicians in a conference, or news of someone they know on maternity leave, it fosters a feeling of connection and a reminder that your organisation's work is affected continually by the choices of others, over which we often have little or no influence and control. But we need to understand and work with them. Team meetings are not only for catching up with in-house matters, nor just about hard information: whilst colleagues will no doubt share project and programme news as appropriate, the chief executive has a particular vantage point in terms of what the buzzwords are, where the power flows are going and where your organisation needs to adjust and align. It is a valuable linguistic challenge to find the words that make your observations relevant as widely as possible to colleagues and to share them regularly. If you can, always end with the implications for everyone. If, in a large organisation, internal communications are dispersed and not directly in your control, you might want to dictate that 'The wider world' or similar is a standing item on any internal information sharing meeting and charge senior managers leading such sessions with including their own information 'from outside' and any snippets from you and the rest of the senior management team.

Secondly, lest I seem to have neglected actual delivery in discussing external relationships, there is no room for softness in agreements around any joint work with partners and contractors, however much people and negotiation skills are a good foundation for this. It is common for shared delivery of a programme to become less than effective over time, with contractors and external collaborators becoming almost colleagues and what should be a contract deteriorating into a fluffy and over-accommodating partnership. Reviewing existing key external protocols, whether they are memoranda of understanding, partnership agreements, delivery contracts or something else, is useful early on. The management tool at your disposal in such circumstances is an organisation-wide approach to procurement, joint working and tendering and re-tendering for contracts. These are all basic organisational good practice to be fine-tuned for your circumstances, and can be overseen operationally at a level below chief executive. In the audit committee, deciding it is time to go out to tender for internal audit services rarely generates emotion. Contrast that with asking a colleague to do the same with an external contract for a longstanding key project, delivered with a person he or she has come to know well: your colleague may actually well feel closer to this external partner than to many internal colleagues, because they have worked on something together at a deep level of detail, perhaps even defended its life together within their respective organisations. The point you will need to establish and maintain is that *all* external arrangements must serve the business and serve it effectively. You may need to lead from the front and demonstrate the 'art of the difficult conversation'.

Thirdly, don't let a gap open up between your organisation's PR and communications and the strategic or policy messages you are beginning to convey externally as chief executive, with partners and stakeholders. There are risks both ways here: you might be beginning to signal a change in direction externally but perhaps informally, knowing that partners are moving on an issue, but you are ahead of your organisation's corporate communications, thus triggering questioning externally of how much of a shift is actually happening. Alternatively, communications might jump ahead of what you can say face to face, and may be read by people who have heard you maintaining the current party line. Always check in with your communications team and invest in its understanding of the underlying issues, not just the communication headlines.

You will have a sense of timing in those issues which are hot topics in your sector, and these of course need the most care. An iconic issue in forestry is the question of what is to be done with our fluffy friends the grey and chewing squirrels, to protect the investment in young trees which is jeopardised by their ability to 'ring' (aka kill) young oaks and other species. Just breaking the bark all round the trunk, in a ring, will kill a tree. A humane and effective approach to controlling numbers is needed, but PR and communications may not be ready for the shift, knowing how much support there is from the wider public for the grey squirrel. As chief executive, you might know of successful communications on a similar difficult issue and you might do well to share that with colleagues, to boost confidence that you can go more public on a contentious issue at the right time.

A wider communications dimension particularly relevant to charities, but important to all organisations, is making sure that external communication by colleagues is not all directed towards the supporter base, if that makes all messaging unhelpfully simplistic in tone and/or content. The fundraising and communication function can often sit closely together or even be carried out by one person. The risk here is that you as chief executive, with your senior team, will be developing and delivering a broader and deeper set of messages, including product development, wider sectoral issues and shifts in delivery but this is under-represented or even completely absent from your established external messaging, conducted by someone who is not involved in or appraised of your developmental work. Messaging can become repetitive and simplistic accounts of need and a call to give, or get involved. This challenge is writ large as I write this, due to public and political noise about charities not respecting their supporters. In the end charities do exist for their causes but they must be seen to be honourable to their supporters, not using them as a means to an end. More established donors will welcome a less basic message. There should always be digestible, accurate, honest and yet appropriately sophisticated information from the organisation. It is the chief executive, with the board, who maintains this balance of 'hitting them between the eyes' and 'informing them between the ears' communications.

Finally, when under pressure we tend to batten down the hatches, just when we most need to reach out. In the UK, the downturn of 2008 meant that many companies and organisations had to focus internally to survive and most found their external partners doing the same. There was a particular danger of insularity and a loss of contact and networking. Such a drawing-in makes responsiveness to your market more difficult, results in life being more boring and reduces opportunities for collaboration, just when you might need them most. When there is stress in your own organisation or a partner organisation, it is especially important to maintain a level of external contact, possibly both *more* formal and focussed than before (emails should probably get shorter in a recession, because the reader in a shrunk organisation has perhaps 140% more to do than before) and also *less* formal (make time to take the pressure off, for example by going for a drink after work with a key collaborator). Advocacy and representation mean very many and varied things, from great fun to pure drudgery, but it should always be in the chief executive's calendar, in the most appropriate form for the circumstance.

Chapter 10

Staying well: your own happiness, health and well-being

This chapter shares reflections on how a chief executive can maintain her or his physical, mental and wider health and well-being: burnout, stress and boredom are the stuff of senior management manuals and indeed the unhappy experience of some. But, just to make the point at the outset, if we substitute 'burnout' with simple 'exhaustion', this, and stress, and especially physical sickness are of course by no means the preserve of the better-paid, management tier. Crowded early morning buses and tubes into our big cities, full of the truly and chronically weary, are reminder enough of the grind of the lower paid: the lucky few who are seriously senior tend to have better hours, less sleep disruption (despite what they might say about 'sleepless nights') and considerable opportunity to keep well and happy. So this chapter assumes basic gratitude for the senior person's lot, rather than special pleading or whingeing.

It is true, though, that any chief executive is in danger of depletion as time goes on and (until you leave, which at some point you should) you need to find ways which work for you to stay well, happy and good at the job. How does such depletion show itself, at this level? It is likely to be a potent combination of the physical (not helped by too much sitting and computer work, however well-adjusted your 'settings'), the emotional and relational and (in its widest sense, rather than the bookish) the intellectual. It is demanding to keep being the person providing impetus and solutions in a team which is embattled, or not replete with energy itself. It is intellectually enervating to be long enough in the same sector to see the same buzzwords, reinvented, come round again and feel the lessons have not been learned from before. One can rather readily become a 'boring old git' to use a friend's carefully chosen phrase, asserting that there is nothing new under the sun and that 'innovative' stuff posited by young people who have never balanced a budget is bound to get nowhere. Defend us from think tanks and jargon, we mutter. But we must not hold on to attitudes which no longer serve us and hold us back, any more than we should have a house full of items that are neither useful or beautiful, to reference William Morris. At work as at home, staying fresh and decluttered may involve helping ourselves and also getting help from others. I once heard of a 75 year old Moroccan woman who presented in pain at a hospital. At the age of 35, she had had an ectopic pregnancy, in which the foetus began to grow in her fallopian tubes and then burst from them. It attached itself to her abdominal organs from whence it fed. Very unusually, he went to full-term. Inevitably and sadly he was not born alive, but, again unusually, remained in her abdomen for 40 years, becoming calcified, as hard as chalk. He was only removed, with careful detachment from the organs through dangerous surgery, all those years later. In the mother's culture it was believed that the baby had gone to sleep and would one day wake. Apart from trying and failing to grasp the reality of this four-decade experience for the mother, I am haunted by this story as a metaphor, applicable both personally and organisationally, of how what was once alive can become rock within us, threatening our very selves and how we are yet tempted, because of myths we weave around ourselves, to give it a home.

Fortunately we can resist ossifying in thought, ideas, hopes and inspirations. Continuing – or starting – to read, listen and participate (TED talks, YouTube, LinkedIn groups, the Harvard Business Review) are all likely to be part of this. I became a chief executive through a degree of flair and a greater degree of good fortune, not because of being well-read on the matter; far from it. Indeed, my hope is that this book will be a useful addition to the relatively small library for aspiring chief executives, as opposed to the many volumes on management and leadership more generically. On your way to becoming a chief executive, or once there, however, read at least some of the literature, along with the biographies of people doing interesting things and the obituaries of people with who led brave and often unpredictable lives. Clock the forms of setbacks and mistakes which have been the forges of their achievements. Read what politicians did after their inevitable failures (and how much their hobbies and family made happiness possible). It almost doesn't matter what you read within this library and where you are on the spectrum between psychobabble and apparently objective texts full of numbers and management techniques. To quote Eleanor Roosevelt again, 'What counts, in the long run, is not what you read; it is what you sift through your own mind; it is the ideas and impressions that are aroused in you by your reading. It is the ideas stirred in your own mind, the ideas which are a reflection of your own thinking, which make you an interesting person'. The more you read, the more videos you watch, the more you'll find what supports you. Biography of a wide range of people is a rich seam, in my view, taking us deeply into personal and wider worlds. Film and poetry are similarly widening of our sense of travel and yet a common human experience.

On the more embodied front, most successful and resilient chief executives are reasonably fit and active in my experience, otherwise it is simply too tiring to do the job. I'm not sure of the causal direction of this: it might be that most successful people are good at looking after themselves anyway and it contributes to their success. Then, because they enjoy a level of fitness (I don't mean necessarily working out, but regularly enjoying physical activity), they are more effective. It goes both ways. Rudy Giuliani, describing in 'Leadership' (Hyperion 2002), his account of his time as Mayor of New York, says that it was particularly on the days when he had a big event that he would go for a swim early in the morning. There is indeed a feeling of being invigorated yet at ease with oneself which you get after a few lengths (and I'm not a great swimmer). You will find what exercise works for you. I have found that skeletal and joint issues which arise in middle age are really not helped by sitting and are not, in my case, susceptible to one major medical magic wand. But the right spinal twists done for long enough and regularly have made it possible, for example, to write this book with relative comfort. I would never, in my 20s, when I once ran from Canterbury to York, and had three children whilst going through a post-viral fatigue period, have imagined the relief from knowing that lying in a weird position lifts the pressure off my sacroiliac joint, but so it is. The project to discover that this is so has been of interest. Any interesting and productive project outside work is good. One that helps you work is SO good.

Another aspect of daily self-awareness as a chief executive is that you are the most likely person in the team to be consciously shaping the rhythms of each 24 hours, from waking to taking to your bed. You are definitely not working all the time but are rather in control and conscious of the balance between work and not, resting and acting, being sedentary and moving, standing and sitting, speaking and being silent, thinking and being in reverie. You may imagine I am in deep reflection on weighty management matters when in quietude. In fact, there is that sign round my neck: 'Sometimes I sits and thinks... and sometimes I just sits'. Henri Poincare, a French mathematician, developed a working method that specifically included deliberately stopping consciously trying to find the solution to a problem, and trusting his 'back brain' to do the work. Any exercise which shifts your brainwaves into a less conscious and data-processing mode is particularly good for these occasions. Such ability to inject mental and physical variety into each day is the best way to avoid decreasing energy over time and once you develop the habit of being conscious about your 24 hour patterns it is not so difficult to tweak them if you need to. For example in the UK from November to February, when energy levels tend to dip in line with daylight hours, you will need to keep yours up, even if it's just a brisk walk round the block on a cold evening; you can't really afford to lapse into a winter somnolence. (Message to self: swim more this winter).

This approach contradicts the increasingly outdated view that in a 'high-powered' job you effectively sublimate everything to it. Quite the reverse; it is the self-aware balancing of work with everything else which singles you out as a pre-eminent leader. This is an issue for men and for women; as I write this chapter, Hillary Clinton is just finishing her time as Secretary of State in the US. Providing compelling evidence that her aides have, truly, attempted to *counter* Einstein's aphorism: 'Not everything that counts, can be counted, and not everything which is counted, counts', we are told with pride that she travelled 956,733 miles, ate 570 airplane meals, visited 112 different countries and held 1700 meetings with world leaders. Missing from this list is, perhaps, the number of strategic global issues she detoxified or indeed progressed; a smaller number we presume, given its absence from the list of big numbers. She did however travel with a bottle of Tabasco sauce lest those 570 meals were too bland, which I salute, as a Tabasco fan myself. We cannot underestimate how much good the reliable supply of the chilli sauce did for her, even if it didn't quite achieve world peace. You may have an equivalent stash of physical or virtual goodies which reminds of you home, helps you enjoy the day and says to you quite unambiguously that you are not a management machine, but a human being.

As well as physical exercise and excavating mental equanimity, I have found it essential to remain fully open to the people and issues outside work which matter to me, when they need me. A good chief executive has days when he or she will walk out of a meeting if a call comes through from someone important to them who is having a truly bleak time. I would go so far as to contest the view that to be a good chief executive you have to be totally present during the whole working day, every day. You should have created a culture around you where it's perfectly fine for anyone, including the chief executive, to say to colleagues on occasion that they might be distracted or interrupted, because there is something serious going on at home or with a friend. This is simply being human. At the weekends, I have days when the phone is tucked away and I am able to indulge in film and reading, having done the intense family years. This is very restorative for me and important, especially as I get older, when I have needed to be more attuned to the different kinds of energy I need, physical, emotional, relational, intellectual, and how to feed them. If you are lucky enough to have children, or other people depending on you in some way, even if the exhaustion risk is high, they are also very helpful in terms of keeping a balance; there is scant chance that you can be truly self-absorbed and potentially lose perspective – which we can do, when we begin to believe that today's work issues really do trump everything else. Or perhaps I am being over-optimistic here; you hear too often of both fathers and mothers with grown up children trying to make up for lost time. Let that not be you, if you are a parent.

For myself, when I somehow lapse into an over-preoccupation with my main work role and begin to neglect other relationships and responsibilities, I am more likely to feel isolated and less authentically me, which has a knock-on effect on how I am at work. I have always been better in my main role if I have other professional responsibilities or structured interests and keep active in things I care about, beyond work. I currently chair TREE AID, which alleviates poverty and the effects of climate change in the Sahel region of Africa through afforestation, community tree planting and associated businesses. A non-executive position, if your primary role allows it, is highly desirable. It gives you experience of a related field; it increases your empathy for the role of the chair and board; it will benefit you in moving on to another role in the future; it increases your productivity in your paid role, of necessity. If chairing a body or being a trustee doesn't fit with your current role then consider training as a coach or acquiring some other flexible skill so that you can pursue that, to suit your diary. All this is predicated on you not having personal duties which preclude such things: even then, something which is not family and not the paid job is desirable, perhaps a very stately progress through a modular distance learning course, either on something close to work or something as far removed from it as possible. I developed yoga fairly consistently over a period of years when I was otherwise engrossed in the physicality of the English landscape – and budgets.

The years do slip by without you realising it and I should admit that I have been a little feeble in maintaining some things I previously enjoyed (such as reading fiction) and equally in recognising that I needed new kinds of activity. It is a very obvious point, but we assume chief executive roles at a certain point in our personal lives, sometimes when family responsibilities are quite preoccupying. We can be so caught up with making a success of our efforts, professionally, that we forget to take stock of what our mortal frames might need at this point in our lives to keep well, in every way, and also how the job might allow or not allow for this. One chief executive was surprised at how much emotion he felt when talking to me about the memory of singing in a choir. Work life had not allowed this to continue. What was it that brought tears as he talked about no longer singing? How could he adapt his week so that this precious activity could be enjoyed again? He longed for the opening of the lungs, and not in order to steer anything, just to blend, just to hold the line…

Is it arguable that as chief executive, your schedule be so flexible, in fact, that you can compress your week, to give you what you feel is a viable work-non-work balance? Is a chief executive allowed more of this than other people? A deputy chief executive once told me, very slightly sardonically, 'Jane (the chief executive) never works every other Friday.' 'How so?' I asked. 'Because she's Jane', he said. He clearly felt he couldn't have had such a regular arrangement. Jane might have said in her defence: 'Well, I've worked more hours than anyone else this week and to take this job I had to live far from my family – it's not sustainable for me otherwise and I'm doing a good leadership job'. I have a lot of sympathy for this but there is something about a regular day not being worked one day in ten which was understandably grating on the colleague. It is normal at chief executive level for the hours worked not to be calculated – I don't particularly agree with that, where there is a strict counting regime for everyone else, but the point is that the role must get done, and you are not free to clock off or be unavailable at your convenience. When you are on holiday, other people have to be ready to cover for you (and this will be on urgent matters) and the same applies for regular days off. What are the deals on your colleagues' side? It will of course seem to them that you do have quite considerable privileges, not least your salary. Perhaps the deputy chief executive in this example would have been more sympathetic to a less privileged colleague wanting flexible hours around a young family? As with so many things, your authority on the issue depends on your wider behaviour, and the quality of communication of such decisions. If you are never working at a certain time, others regularly have to step in if there is something you would usually do. How is such flexibility shown throughout the organisation and if all senior managers wanted a similar arrangement could it be accommodated? Or for everyone? If it is unpaid is it more acceptable? This is an area where the values of the organisation are practical tools. If one of those is no privilege based on seniority, then you will gain much respect by not privileging yourself and making arrangements as conducive as possible to those with other responsibilities and lower salaries.

A related issue is having working days out of the office, to have thinking time or to do complex pieces of work. If you feel you need time out to have a break from all the demands and it's essentially a sanity mechanism, you need to try to de-escalate the pressures: days out would only be an interim measure in any stress management programme you might put in place with a colleague, so it should not be a long-term part of your working life. More positively, Frances, who heads a very large national body and is an introvert by personality type, loves her 'cardigan days'. At home she does not have to be in role, drinks her own coffee and can focus on reflecting, thinking and planning. Here again, clarity about your availability on these days (perhaps only urgent communication, through your PA?), their frequency and whether there are parallel arrangements for others all put this option on a fair and well-understood footing. In some organisations, working from home is encouraged but in others it reduces cohesion too much: you will have to work out what is sensible for your business and colleagues and, again, act fairly, with a bias to those who have fewer privileges in general.

So, to summarise this chapter and indeed echo a recurring theme of the book: showing that you are not a machine is all to the good. Crucially, as chief executive, you then need to show that you are more *effective* through looking after yourself and what matters to you than if you did indeed pretend to be an automaton. This is good for your colleagues to see. From your perspective, your professional self-knowledge extends to how you protect your well-being. This builds your resilience for the 'ends of a plank' times, protects your most important relationships (which are not usually at work) and makes a 'falling off the cliff' career moment less likely. But you have to be fair to others when you make any adjustments at work to accommodate your well-being. I hope you do indeed stay very well and are very happy, at work and beyond.

Chapter 11

Leaving: Transitioning with poise

This final chapter needs something of a caveat, in that it deals primarily with the normal run of departures, that is, ones that are planned or within your expected timeframe for moving, or arising out of having landed an irresistible new job unexpectedly. Having to leave, because of difficult personal circumstances or things coming to an end in a way which you did not wish, such as being sacked or being made redundant, is in another category. These difficult experiences are life events more than work events and their impact on your self-esteem and health can be great, requiring all the attention and support of any unexpected change and loss. As with moving on to a new role in more positive circumstances, you should ask yourself what you really need at this time and how to get there, perhaps avoiding assuming it is either more of the same or an utterly different life. It is just that this is harder to do when you've had a body blow: there is so much fear and anxiety when change is not of your choosing and you may want to find someone to talk with whom you can trust, possibly who's been through it, and maybe find professional support too, to help form a good base for looking at future options.

Returning to the less complex territory of more usual departures, experienced and intuitive leaders I have spoken with tend to have an internal clock, which tells them it is time to move on. They will say in a pretty matter of fact way, 'Ten years just feels too long in an academic leadership position,' or, 'After three years, you're becoming less effective and you really need to go by five.' Of course, there are no generalisations and, anyway, real life intervenes. In my own case, I thought five years was about right in my last role but left after nearly nine, due to a downturn which meant relative risk for the organisation as well as fewer external roles to look at. There was also the inherent reward and enjoyment of the post, but this happily common experience has to be regarded as potentially a false friend, inducing inertia and stagnation. Apparent loyalty and doggedness might be a cover for not doing the right thing for you or the organisation, for less good reasons. Luckily I seem to be one of those people who cogitates about and anticipates change; then when it happens I am ready for it and get on with it without procrastination. This is behaviour a chief executive is likely to have shown during a time in post on a number of issues, particularly restructures, and it serves you well for the end of your time in a role.

I was once on the board of a small organisation where the top of the risk register was always the departure of the lead executive. This is not a sign of a strong business. Senior departures are normal events; such departures can be opportunities and the attendant risks should be mitigated. There are many reasons why it is good not to stay indefinitely. The chances that the organisation's needs match the skills you had when you arrived will be diminishing as you effect the change that was required early on and for which, on appointment, you were assessed: you are fortunate if there is 80% convergence, not divergence, between your offer and the organisation's needs after three to five years. Additionally, all being well you will be maturing and shifting your interests, for example developing a passion for small business start-ups, when eight years ago you might have been a leader in digital media. Or you might now have less energy for a start-up and be more attracted by a consolidation role. You might fancy working with a smaller team, or a bigger one, for the different skills you would need to develop. For a while, you can sublimate these changing interests, but if you stall indefinitely there will be a cost to your verve – and your pride in yourself when you're retired and wonder if you could have taken a risk and experienced more.

You will also find it harder, over time, to avoid operating within your comfort areas and accepting the constraints of your team, rather than challenging them. A chief executive of a small local authority, where he or she has to bring in a particular skill, might be very good at bringing in investment, but have little time for or interest in 'bog standard' services, such as waste collection (definitely a strategic, or as I prefer it, long-term and important, area). For a number of years it is fine to bring in that expertise around him or her. But over time, chief executive attention has to be sufficiently focused on core, if mundane, business. Or perhaps the reverse: someone who is excellent at operations may not be the right person to bring in major new investment when it is needed. A natural balancing will need to take place, especially where the demands of a post are wide and may not be easily met in one person. The same applies in the external, stakeholder relationships: if there is not much churn in these networks and things basically function fine, it's hard to name the collective stagnation, the unhealthy mutual reinforcement of shared strengths and ways of doing things which make it more likely that challenges are not met, opportunities not taken. An eye for when change is needed is a responsibility of leadership and can sometimes only be addressed by introducing fairly disruptive change. This can include, radically, removing yourself from the equation; never assume that the blocks are only elsewhere.

So to the actual leaving of a role. As I write this a chief executive friend is trying to steel herself to hand in her notice, essentially to take (slightly) early retirement. She's been successful, she's got a lot else that she'd be brilliant at, she will have enough money, she's feeling stressed and her son wants her to do it for her own well-being. But she's finding it hard to send the email. The forces of inertia are strong in all of us and her fears of losing her current identity – and living on a greatly reduced salary – are reasonable enough. As with many decisions, there is a moment when you can do it and for some people it will take a long time to get to this point. This applies at much earlier career points than retirement and in fact I have seen a good number of young people very attached to their first or second 'proper' workplace, because of all the opportunities, learning and rich working relationships it has given them, for the first time in their working lives. Stalling at this stage of career is even more risky than when you are dithering about taking early retirement.

All I would say is that if you are beginning not to feel too upbeat in your role and have a growing sense of unease about where you are, then this should be enough evidence that there is something better for you. Always hold in your mind the 'What else, what better?' question: something is waiting to reveal itself, even as you anticipate the losing of the role. Try to be quite specific about this even if your new role is unlikely to meet all your needs. It might be a change in subject matter, perhaps personnel, perhaps a different working environment, culturally or intellectually. Often I hear people say, 'I still believe in the business, but it's what we have to do to deliver it which is getting me down'. Probably every business and sector has idiocies in its business models, but a change is as a good as a rest, up to a point. Try to imagine other benefits of your departure: the space you are creating for others to progress into, or not having to do the same journey in every day – whatever it is which, for you, beckons towards a better future. And then act, bearing in mind some factors discussed below.

Sometimes of course an opportunity comes up unexpectedly and you feel you have to go for it. This can result in a relatively sudden departure of the chief executive, with no time on either side for cogitating about the perfect moment, although one hopes that there is a business continuity plan thread about what would happen in the absence of a chief executive. In this case, I would counsel giving careful consideration to when and how you might tell your chair. There is an argument not to tell her or him until you are offered the job, because you don't want to reveal less than 100% commitment. If it upsets them that the first they hear is that you've chosen another role above the current one, well, you are going, so, you might argue, it makes no odds. There is a lot of logic in this, although the counter-argument is that if the relationship with the chair has basically been good and open, it should be able to tolerate an earlier heads-up and then it can close with trust and openness to the end. This feels a bit different from when you are at more junior levels, as the stakes for the organisation are higher.

As a chair, I can say it helps to have the headspace to get used to the idea and begin to plan what will need to be done if the new job is, indeed, offered to 'your' departing chief executive. I would not interpret the news as a loss of commitment to the role, unless there was actual evidence of this in performance. Remember as a chief executive that the biggest single responsibility a chair has is the recruitment of your successor. It takes a lot of time and thought and is usually done by a group of volunteers, led by the chair, who may have a lot else on. Even if there is a recruitment agency it will need managing. The chair will have invested in one relationship and will be aware that they will need to put time and relational energy into a new one. A chief executive will show respect and empathy in communicating early with the chair, in my view, even if it is a time when you are understandably pretty self-preoccupied. But you may feel that your relationship does not merit this or would not be helped by it. Just make a conscious decision.

Occasionally the external environment and wider circumstances mean it is (despite my earlier comments about indispensability often being overstated) genuinely risky if the chief executive moves and you should bear that in mind: do you have a responsibility to stay at that moment, whatever the new offer? (There is also an element of self-interest here, in that the organisation could suffer and your legacy be impaired, if you leave at that point). To be honest, there will be lots of occasions when you could quite legitimately put on your cv that you 'completed a restructure' and 'continued to secure funding', whilst knowing that the organisation still faces another risk you were recruited to face, or that the outcomes of your actions have not yet fully bedded in. Whether you go at a time of risk will depend on how you rate the value of the current organisation (to you and more widely) versus that of the new one; and of course how high you put personal opportunities and needs, in the ranking of considerations about how you should act in this kind of situation. Your well-being is your number one responsibility because, without this, you are useless. How you interpret this business of looking after yourself, and for what purpose, is at the heart of many of the most interesting conversations in the world. Put simply, conventional notions of 'duty' and 'responsibility' play less strongly with some people than with others.

For the team, it is likely that the departure of the chief executive is the biggest single uncertainty it will face, apart from a drastic downsizing, merger or closure. All you can and should do is to be straightforward as soon as you know. As with moving on earlier in your career at more junior levels, you should not make it public if no contracts have been signed, but you may want to inform your PA, so that they don't feel as I suggested a chair may feel in the same situation, above, and can handle any awkward requests from external contacts for meetings in seven months' time. From the outset it is good to have formulated a succinct, one line story about why you are going and to make sure that it conveys ongoing confidence in the organisation and its skills. When I did a planned departure from a team of about 20, within which I directly managed about 25%, the chair and I choreographed the telling with care, so that those for whom I was their manager knew the day before: I felt this respected the closer ties I had with them and meant they had a day to assimilate the news and be relatively accustomed to it the next day. To avoid a long gap between chief executives, we had to contract with a recruitment agency before the team knew. The board was aware but did not allude to it with the team.

If you have been in an organisation a reasonable length of time, you could well have had some oblique or direct questions from colleagues about your thoughts on how long you will be around. (If it has been possible to say with any degree of accuracy, you will have talked with the chair about how long you expect to stay). Only you know how you best handle these conversations with colleagues, whose tolerance of change and uncertainty (and their basic rating of you as a boss!) will vary. But like every situation, the worst you can do is say something that turns out to be misleading. For most of us, saying that we won't be there for ever is surely uncontroversial (unless we are truly the least dynamic boss, with retirement far on the horizon and precious few job opportunities). In my case, I once said on being asked the question by colleagues, 'I would not go if I felt the organisation was at risk', which implies the converse, that I might go if I felt it was not at risk; that message was I think heard, although the timing can surprise anyone.

Other considerations about timing include:

- Where your organisation is in the strategic cycle. Going too late when a new strategic period is imminent is potentially unfair for a new chief executive, who has to lead the creation of the next strategy without much lived knowledge. But if you go just when you have finalised a strategy, you are requiring someone to pick up something that they were not involved in. They may be grateful that it is there, however, if it needed your credibility with stakeholders and funders. Only you and the chair can judge this one in your case, but obviously midway through a strategic period can make a lot of sense, if you have the option.

- Terms of office of your chair and key board members: if you have a choice, avoiding leaving just before your chair goes is fairer to everyone.

- Likely plans of key senior colleagues and any particular organisational weaknesses if there is a vacancy in one of these roles, as well as in that of the chief executive.

- Major funding and investment cycles, especially those which rely on the chief executive to land them.

- Your personal circumstances and how much appetite you have for change at this time. When Biden, in the USA, announced that he was reviewing whether he would run for the Democratic Presidential nomination in 2016, he said he was uncertain whether he had the heart for it, as his son had died of cancer earlier in the year. I found this a helpful public acknowledgement of the weight and weariness of grief and how those things that once seemed important now fail to stir the belly. Imagine doing an election rally when all you want to do is crawl up and bawl. We have our equivalents.

By the time you are considering leaving a chief executive role, and looking around for what next, you will should have a pretty sound sense of your professional self and what kind of role is likely to be fulfilling for you. However all the comments made much earlier in the book about not confining yourself in roles which are *too* comfortable for your personality still apply. I declined one role which made sense on paper for me as a next move but which felt too conservative, a bit of a cul de sac. It is never too late to push the boundaries. As I write, I am not currently an organisational chief executive, and my strapline is that I am 'resting myself and testing myself': enjoying not taking the weight of an organisation on my shoulders every day but also seeing if I can live without the rewards, the salary, the sense of being well occupied without having to create each day from scratch. I felt I needed to check my dependencies. Of course, leadership seems to follow a leader, even if she is trying to lay it down, and that is something to reflect on, making sure that accepting a leadership role in whatever guise, after a formal role has been laid down, is not out of need.

When I left my last role I made a simple criteria list for whatever I did next, which included:

- being slightly or significantly scary
- being involved in issues not addressed by many others
- introducing me to new and interesting people
- being good for me physically and intellectually.
- involving more water, as I missed that somewhat, being based in the Midlands of the UK.

In this phase in my life, I knew I wanted to learn some new skills, have the option to think about my own thoughts rather than respond to emails quite so much, befriend London, having been an outsider, read more for pleasure and expand my social and intellectual worlds. I needed to relax into the period in which I would become decisively middle-aged, a time when possibly one becomes naturally more inner and reflective. I also needed to earn enough money to live and even my period of openness is in danger of being programmed. Still, my Twitter account said I was 'walking, watching and writing', which is about as specific as I have wanted to be as this process unfolded.

When we do have more space to get reacquainted with ourselves, we might discover we are not much different from the self we knew already, echoing Frances' earlier point about us, in the end, having to operate within our own personalities, not suddenly becoming Steve Jobs if there has never been an inkling of us being that kind of person. I thought I'd do more team games for example, but, oh the manifold reasons I devise about why I can't make frisbee in Hyde Park on Sundays! Walking, yoga and cycling are still bubbling up however, as an important part of who I am, just in a different setting; and a few boundaries have been, if not pushed, at least leant against: I have made some websites and achieved a start-up and certainly opened up new circles of friends and acquaintances at a time when these can tend to stagnate. It's fascinating to see how much you change when there are not too many reasons stopping you – probably a disappointing amount, but the small shifts are rewarding. I have done less well in reducing the email flow and I have not been in water enough. I could still push my fear boundaries further. I include these thoughts in this book not to imply that reorientation only has relevance for chief executives; far from it. But it is particularly important for leaders to pay attention to these pivotal life points and not to be out of date about who we really are and what we need, because the leader with few delusions about themselves (there will always be some) will draw others to him or her and withstand better the inevitable minor – or major – assaults on the self which leadership implies.

So, I have started a new project from scratch and moved home, although there have also been helpful continuities, in my pro bono roles and of course friends and family. Whilst initiating what is definitely a change, it has been important not to rule anything out, including eventually a return to a salaried role, with the intention of doing it better, having peered further into my gifts and shortcomings and what the rest of my life might usefully be about. Being radically open means not having very specific answers to the question: 'So what are you going to do next?' and sometimes I have had to carry other people's concern or disappointment. One person said: 'But you've always been my role model with your career!' as if it confused their image of me as a professional (not one I carried of myself particularly) for me to withdraw a bit and regroup (however good a pedigree this has in refreshing life, from Buddha to defeated politicians). It is also sometimes easier to manage the message of the chief executive's departure if he or she moves to a bigger, more prestigious, role – which I did not, in this instance – and if you ever, similarly, leave to have an interesting but hard-to-summarise change of tack, it is good to give a helpful line on what you are up to, especially for the chair, who may be quizzed about why you are going and where. In the end, however, you must do what is right for you and let other people deal with it.

If you are moving on to a new chief executive role, it is not so different a leaving process from that which you have done before, with possibly more claims on your time from the new place, and more farewells, encroaching on your final weeks at your current organisation. At this level, such demands from your future workplace are to be expected, but it is helpful to agree with your current and future chairs whether you will give a day or two back to your current organisation in return, after your successor has started. Compared with taking up your first chief executive role, just a bit more attention needs to be given to choreographing press releases and any public statements, making sure that your organisation is lined up with a positive press release about your successor – if in place, or a positive sentence about recruitment if not – at the same time as he or she is announcing *their* departure and new role. Think of it like the chain in house buying and make sure it all aligns, in communication terms. Your press people need to be proactive on this, making a link to their equivalents. Recruitment procedures and publicity around them constitute one area where organisations' cultural differences show themselves – from control and formality to the other extreme – which can create occasional clunky and potentially embarrassing moments. I was once in a situation where my successor's organisation went public on her move before we had got clearance about the announcement our end, which created a bit of a scramble. There was no culture of clearance in the other organisation and we should have thought of this.

Finally, let's admit that leaving takes energy, for everyone concerned, including your PA, your chair and others. There will be individuals who want that one-to-one goodbye – not always those you expect, either – and many people whom you want to see and say thank you to, too. These can be precious times, with things said which wouldn't otherwise be said and, whether or not you will keep in touch with many people, that rounding off of what you've done together is important and special. However, it needs to be done without encroaching too much on your team and daily business, as far as possible. I have resorted to the physical clearing of my space mostly out of work time, so that in the office I was still somewhat present to the team and able, mostly, to carry on working. If a goodbye period goes on too long it really does get tedious for everyone. You can sense when people have mentally made the shift and are ready now for you to head off so they can start the new regime. Meanwhile there may be more or less in the way of celebrations than what you expected and you might feel a little 'unsighted' on them. Looking back, I think having the right words ready in your back pocket for any moment in the leaving period is not a bad idea.

There are no hard and fast rules about handover but I would say there is responsibility on both sides. An incoming chief executive should say what they need and in what form so that they can work effectively from the outset. This may mean some face to face time along with enough time to go through briefing documents and ask questions. Similarly, the outgoing chief executive is entitled to give attention to leaving the information he or she thinks is needed, even if his or her successor does not seem very interested. Where an outgoing chief executive seems unwilling to share information, or the incoming chief executive seems disinterested, it is sensible to ask the chair to oil the wheels. Caution is advisable about how much a new chief executive is in the office with the outgoing one; after a certain point it can become confusing to colleagues and I think best to keep it limited and to choreograph it carefully.

So, the desk is tidy, auto-reply is on, there is a neat file of current issues and contacts for whoever comes next, but long email chains have been consigned to the bin. The thank you gifts have been delivered or left on your colleagues' desks. You put the final houseplant you are taking with you into your final carrier bag and you go. At this time of transition (better than calling it simply ending), you breathe out and take care of the most important matters in your life. I tend to belong to the 'shake the sand off your sandals' school and give plenty of space for my successor, along with the offer of a phone call any time on matters that needs it. What good fortune to have so many moments to remember, enough to regret and learn from, and a few good relationships that may persist. Onwards.

Lightning Source UK Ltd.
Milton Keynes UK
UKHW020625010621
384721UK00003B/59